THE WORLD AS I REMEMBER IT:

Through the Eyes of a Ragamuffin

MULTNOMAH

THE WORLD AS I REMEMBER IT

Published in association with Eames Literary Service, Nashville, Tennesee.

International Standard Book Number: 978-1-60142-721-2

Cover and interior design by Brand Navigation, LLC,
Benjamin Kinzer, Bill Chiaravalle and Terra Petersen. www.brandnavigation.com

Published in the United States by Multnomah, an imprint of the Crown Publishing Group, a division of Penguin Random House LLC, New York.

MULTNOMAH® and its mountain colophon are registered trademarks of Penguin Random House LLC.

146087801

Contents

Welcome

THANK YOU FOR SHARING AN APPRECIATION OF the writings of Rich Mullins. Rich had a way with words, and a collection of his writings seems an appropriate tribute to a man who has been referred to as "the greatest songwriter of our time." Rich is gone from this earth, but will never be forgotten.

Rich had moved to the Southwest to live among Native American people and begin a work among them. Rich expressed concern that our very neighbors are overlooked while we help others far away. Rich went to learn first, then teach. He believed we have a lot to learn from the rich culture and awareness of God that Native people can teach us. He hoped to live Christ rather than tell about Him.

So that the work he began and hoped to do on Native American reservations can continue, a not-for-profit foundation is being established. The Legacy of Kid Brothers of St. Frank will exist to help bring the arts, in the spirit and love of Christ, to children and adults living on the reservations. St. Francis' teachings on obedience, chastity, service, and the dignity of the poor will serve as guidelines for this foundation, as they did for Rich and Beaker, the founders of Kid Brothers of St. Frank. At the time this is written, the foundation's formation is underway. If you would like more information, you may write to The Legacy of Kid Brothers of St. Frank at P.O. Box 11526, Wichita, Kansas 67202, and information will be sent as soon as it is available.

I ask, as you read the writings and enjoy the scenes, that you think not of the man who penned them, but rather of the God about whom he wrote. I will miss Rich until I see him again. Until then, I rejoice in the fact that he is home.

Jim Dunning

Jim Dunning

Richard Mullins' Manager

The World as I Remember It

When I leave I want to go out l

And when I lea

Going Home

It'll be like candlelight in Central Park

And it won't break my heart t

e Elijah

th a whirlwind to fuel my chariot of fire

back on the stars

WHEN RICH MULLINS WENT HOME TO THE LORD, he left behind a spiritual and artistic legacy that touched many. On September 19, 1997, Rich and fellow musician Mitch McVicker were traveling southbound on I-39 near Peoria, Illinois, to a benefit concert in Wichita, Kansas. They lost control of their Jeep and flipped. They were thrown onto the road. The driver of a rig swerved to miss the Jeep, but hit Rich.

say goodbye

McVicker, twenty-four, suffered serious head and internal injuries. Rich was dead at forty-one.

Throughout his career, his dogged grip on what was good and true meant Christians from many different denominations found hope and meaning in his songs and ministry.

Richard Wayne Mullins was born October 21, 1955, in Richmond, Indiana. The third of John and Neva Mullins' six children—four boys and two girls—Rich was raised on his parents' Indiana farm.

Rich's musical training began at an early age. His great grandmother taught him hymns while he learned to play the piano from Mary Kellner. Rich considered Kellner to be one of his greatest musical influences, not only for teaching him how to play and introducing him to the great masters, but also for sparking his passion and imagination about what he was learning. He is said to have written his first song on the piano at age four. As a teenager, he wrote songs while driving a tractor in the fields on his father's farm.

Pictures in the Sky

1987

He graduated from Northeastern High School in 1974. As a student at Cincinnati Bible College, Rich joined Zion Ministries and sang in the pop-vocal quartet Zion. Though he was the only member to pursue music as a vocation, in 1981, the group—through a generous grant from Rich's uncle—independently produced an album, *Behold the Man.* The record, sold almost exclusively at Zion's concerts and long out of print, featured Rich solo on one song, "Heaven in His Eyes." The rest featured either group performances or duets. That same year, the group performed at Nashville's Koinonia Coffeehouse, and Reunion Records' Mike Blanton heard a tape. He soon signed Rich to a publishing deal.

In 1983, Amy Grant recorded Rich's "Sing Your Praise to the Lord" for *Age to Age.* Within a short time, the song was seemingly absorbed into the American hymnody. Grant continued to champion Rich as a writer, recording "Doubly Good to You" for *Straight Ahead* and "Love of Another Kind" for *Unguarded.*

(And I won't lack my heart to say goodbye

Winds of Heaven, Stuff of Earth

1988

Rich signed his first recording contract and released *Rich Mullins*, his debut on Reunion Records (the label founded by Grant's managers) in 1985. The simple cover art indicated his self-deprecating humor, with a cover portrait that included only part of his face and left his name on his T-shirt a tangled mess from behind his folded arms. The album's lyrics portrayed a rare honesty. As Rich sings in "A Few Good Men": Show me a someone who knows how to struggle / Who isn't caught in the hold of his luxuries / I just need to see / Someone who was made for trouble / Who could come and help shape our destiny.

With his second record, *Pictures in the Sky*, Christian music fans began to notice Rich in earnest. "Screen Door" was an unlikely hit (with its *a cappella* doo-wop arrangement and catchy "hand-clap-finger-snap-knee-slap" rhythm) that was very different from usual Christian radio fare. "Verge of a Miracle" was also a success, full of crisp, shimmery sounds and words full of optimism without resorting to platitudes.

With *Winds of Heaven, Stuff of Earth,* Rich learned to express himself in a way that was simpler, yet still had depth. "The Other Side of the World" was a compelling reminder that the Kingdom of God is built by "the least of these." In "If I Stand," he used spare instrumentation to underscore his longing to live a life of faith, grace, and peace. "Awesome God," a simple song expressing the grandest of truths, had the biggest impact: Churches everywhere incorporated the song into their worship, and almost overnight Rich became one of the biggest names in Christian music. While other artists chose to move closer to the inside of the industry, Rich moved away. Having lived in Nashville since the beginning of his career, he moved to Wichita to take part in the ministry of the Reverend Maurice Howard at Wichita's Central Christian Church.

Although Howard passed away a few months after Rich moved to Kansas, Rich stayed on, basing his music and ministry from Central Christian Church. He wanted to coordinate his mission work with his

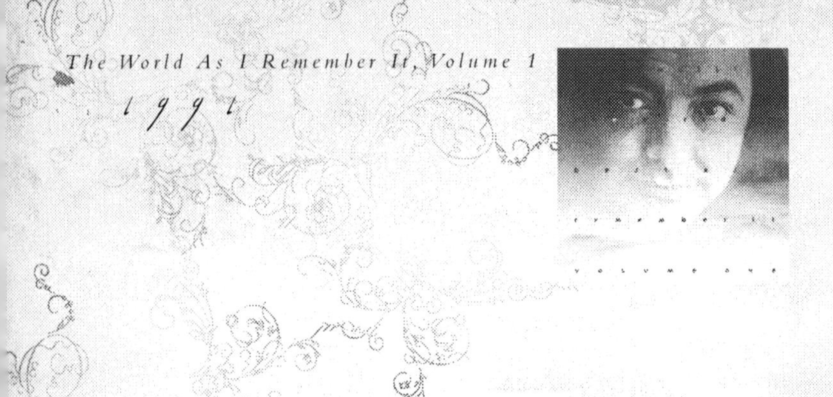

musical career. He moved into a house with lifelong friend and musical collaborator Beaker.

With *Never Picture Perfect*, Rich delved deeper into his musical heritage and personal experience to make art with a universal appeal. "While the Nations Rage" went hand in hand with "The Other Side of the World" challenging Christians to not turn a blind eye to social injustice. "First Family" offered a tribute to his parents. On songs like "My One Thing" and "Hope to Carry On," Rich mixed in folk instruments like Appalachian hammered dulcimer and mandolin, while more driving rock energy began showing up in his music.

While his "celebrity" status continued to rise, Rich often shifted the focus off himself, stepping out of the limelight. He'd often join an audience *before* a show. In rural Missouri, Rich came into the auditorium while the house lights were still up, guitar in hand. "The show's not starting just yet," he said, "but while we're waiting, I wanted to teach you this song we'll be doing later. It's a new one, so you probably

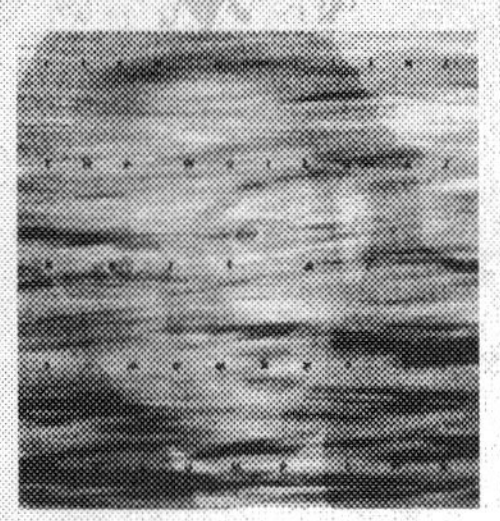

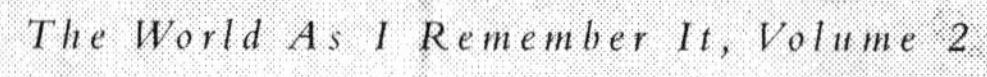

haven't heard it before." Then he took the audience through the chorus to "Sometimes by Step" one line at a time until they had it down.

He toured relentlessly to bring his music to the public. The shows were almost entirely acoustic (years before "unplugged" became a trend) and featured supporting acts as Rich's band, trading off on a multitude of instruments, including hammered dulcimer, accordion, and all manner of ethnic percussion. For the rhythm on "Screen Door," in a marvelous feat of choreography, they employed bar stools and plastic cups. They usually opened the show with a rendition of Handel's "Hallelujah" chorus sung *a cappella* and arranged in the Beach Boys' style.

The spirit of these shows was closely reflected in Rich's two-volume album, *The World As Best As I Remember It.* The first disc opened with the strains of bagpipes and a boy soprano singing the plaintive prayer: O God, You are my God / And I will ever praise You / I will seek You in the morning / I will learn to walk in Your ways / And step by

A Liturgy, A Legacy & A Ragamuffin Band

1 9 9 3

step You'll lead me / And I will follow You all of my days.

Rich expressed on these discs a glimpse not only of the state of the world, but also of himself, from celebrating the incarnation of Christ in "Boy Like Me/Man Like You" or "The Maker of Noses," to the broken spirit longing for eternity in "Calling Out Your Name" and "The River."

During this period, there were rumors of Rich's retirement from music. He often spoke of his interest in being a missionary and teaching music to children. When Beaker married and moved away in 1993, Rich cut back his concert and recording schedule to study music education at Friends University in Wichita. He then moved in with Friends' campus chaplain and theology professor Jim Smith and his family.

For *A Liturgy, A Legacy & A Ragamuffin Band*, Rich retained much of the musical spirit of his previous two records, while drawing on the influences and musical friendships of his "Ragamuffin Band." Each of the members—Jimmy Abegg, Rick Elias, Phil Madeira, Lee

Lundgren, Aaron Smith, and Billy Crockett—had musical careers of their own. The high profile band spread the spotlight around, making Rich less the focus.

The record consisted of two parts: Part one ("the Liturgy") was designed to convey the idea of a liturgy, or an order of worship; part two ("the Legacy") was conceived as an expression of the tension of being a Christian in America.

"Growing up in a non-liturgical church," Rich had said, "we thought we were non-liturgical. But when I look back, we definitely had one. You know, like the Call to Worship, Hymn of Praise, Prayer Hymn, Prayer Time, Offering, Sermon…this thing that we follow. There is something very exciting to me about singing hymns that people have been singing for generations."

He said if we believe in the communion of the saints, then it is not only communion with the saints that are still in the Body, but also with the saints of old. So, he said, it connects us with a lot more people.

In 1995, after receiving his degree in Music Education from Friends University, Rich took a big step: he moved to the reservation near Window Rock, Arizona, to teach music to the children on the Navajo reservation. One of his goals was to organize a choir that might go on the road with him.

His life at Window Rock was represented somewhat on *Brother's Keeper*, his second record with the Ragamuffins. The album featured artwork and photos inspired by and taken on the reservation. It was also the first record where Rich held the producer's credit, shared with the other members of the band.

The words captured a compelling picture of grace and redemption, as in "Wounds of Love": Well, if passion can lead to prayer / Then maybe prayer can give us faith / And if faith is all we got / Then maybe faith is all we need.

Once the record was out, he put that faith to the test, cutting most of his ties to the first decade of his career. He ended his decade-long

relationship with Reunion Records and with his longtime manager. He spent a good deal of time just concentrating on his work in New Mexico and playing a few shows here and there.

Reunion issued *Songs*, featuring many of Rich's biggest hits, plus three new recordings (a remake of Rich's personal favorite, "Elijah," his own recording of the ever-popular "Sing Your Praise to the Lord," and the buried gem "We Are Not As Strong As We Think We Are").

During this independent period, Rich wrote and recorded *Canticle of the Plains*, a musical based on the life and legend of St. Francis of Assisi, set in the American Old West. While most of Rich's records had some underlying theme, this was the first to have a "story" sketched out in the liner notes and fleshed out as a drama. He produced the record with Ragamuffin and This Train bassist Mark Robertson, and wrote the songs with Beaker and Mitch McVicker. However, Rich didn't actually sing on this project; the "parts" were sung by the different cast members. Mitch sang the role

of Frank, a disillusioned veteran of the Civil War, who returns home seeking God's greater plan. Michael Tait sang the role of Buzz, a former slave, anxious to find the meaning of freedom. Kevin Smith portrayed Ivory, a childhood friend of Frank's, intrigued by the change that has come over his friend. Leigh Nash rounds out the cast as Clare, the love who gives Frank up so he can pursue the purpose laid before him by God.

A month before his death, Rich signed a new recording contract with Myrrh Records. He was scheduled to go into the studio in October with Rick Elias to work on *The Jesus Record*, for June 1998. He submitted a demo tape of rough home recordings of the songs to be included on the finished disc.

As a tribute to Rich's legacy, the Ragamuffin Band (headed by producer and guitarist Rick Elias) has recorded and sung the songs themselves to help continue the work Rich began during his lifetime.

There were four memorial services held for Rich. On

September 26, a Nashville service was held at Christ Presbyterian Church. The next day, a service was held at Wichita State University's Henry Levitt Arena with more than five thousand people in attendance. On October 13, a memorial service was held on the reservation in Window Rock, Arizona. Then, on October 15, a final service was held in memory of Rich at the Compassion International headquarters in Colorado Springs, Colorado.

Canticle of the Plains was the last project Rich completed during his life. As with all of Rich's concerts, *Canticle of the Plains* ends with a period of worship to the Father. It is fitting that Rich would leave us with this final admonition to keep our attention and our adoration squarely focused on our Creator, Redeemer, and Inspirer.

Rich told the truth.

And now he is free.

The Columns

1991–1995

For nearly six years, Rich shared his thoughts about faith and life through his columns in *Release*. When his first column was published in Spring of 1991, the editors introduced him this way: "Rich not only has a lot to say…he also has a unique way of saying it. And although Mr. Mullins could easily fit into that intellectual bohemian-type category (we're sure he could hold his own in a discussion with any theologian or philosopher of old) most often, his message is a straightforward call back to the principles of faith. He's a poet, a scholar, a gentleman, and yes, just a little bit off-center. But that's why we like him, and are pleased to welcome Rich to *Release* with this regular column. We trust you'll love him and what he has to say as much as we do…."

Spring

1991

Telling the Joke

The only thing worse than a joke you don't get is the explanation that is bound to follow: an explanation that, while it may help you see why you should have seen the humor that you so lamely missed, is little likely to make you laugh. It may provoke you to muster a sympathy snicker so as to avoid more of an already tedious and misdirected lecture. It may inspire a mild giggle of recognition, but it will hardly ever raise a real belly-laugh, which was the original desired effect.

And so, here I go—me and a dozen thousand other people—trying to explain a joke that we would do better to learn to better tell. I am setting out to explain again why Jesus is the only true hope for the world, why we should put our faith in Him, and what all of that won't mean. I am collecting the information, selecting from what I hope will be usable as evidence, arranging my findings into arguments, framing it for presentation and recognizing that,

while it may all be fine as far as it goes, it doesn't go far enough.

But then I remember two things. The first thing I remember is how I once won an argument with a heathen friend of mine who—after I had whacked away his last scrap of defense, after I had successfully cut off every possible escape route that he could use, after I had backed him into an inescapable corner and hit him with a great inarguable truth—blew me away by simply saying, "I do not *want* to be a Christian. I don't want your Jesus Christ." There was no argument left to be had or won. Faith is a matter of the will as much as it is of the intellect. I wanted to believe in Jesus. My friend wanted to believe in himself. In spite of how convincing my reason was, my reason was not compelling.

So, the second thing I remember is this: I am a Christian because I have seen the love of God lived out in the lives of people who know Him. The Word has become flesh and I have encountered God in the people who have manifested (in many "unreasonable" ways) His Presence; a Presence that is more than convincing—it is a Presence that is compelling. I am a Christian, not because someone explained the nuts and bolts of Christianity to me, but because there were people who were willing to be nuts and bolts, who through their explanation of it, held it together so that I could experience it and be compelled by it to obey. "If I be lifted up," Jesus said, "I will draw all men unto me."

Faith is a matter *of the* will
as much as it is *of* the intellect.
I wanted *to* believe *in* Jesus.

So, here I offer what is possibly the worst thing that can be offered: an explanation of a joke. And, what makes this more inexcusable than the fact that this is that, is the added fact that this is an explanation to a joke you've already gotten. I offer it anyway. I offer it in the hope that it might somehow encourage you to live out your lives and, by your living, tell the joke that I, in my writing, so feebly attempt to explain. Love one another, forgive one another, work as unto God, let the peace of Christ reign in your hearts. Make it your ambition to lead quiet lives. Obey. Greet one another with a holy kiss. No one will argue with that.

And I will keep rattling on about how good it all is and won't expect to be taken too seriously. I and a dozen thousand other bores will fill up book shelves and record bins and magazine racks with writing that is fine as far as it goes—hoping that it will help you somehow to go farther. Much that I have read has challenged my opinion and hardened my convictions—I am thankful for it. It is for you (and for me, more in my living than in my writing) to let our light so shine before men that they may see our good works and glorify our Father in Heaven.

[Note: This column was reprinted in the February/March 1996 issue of *Release*.]

Summer
1991

Considering the Lilies

Did I forget to tell you that He loved lilies? It is a well-known and much overlooked fact of His life—as known and overlooked as the lilies He loved. And it's a puzzling fact, too. Why lilies? Why especially lilies?

Maybe He loved lilies for being white, the way many people love roses for being red. Maybe it was because of the brilliant green of their long, slender stalks or the glorious, darker green of their leaves. Maybe He loved them because their blooms looked like trumpets and their leaves resembled swords. It could have been their simplicity, it might have been their commonness. It may have been because of all of that and it just as easily could have been because of none of that at all. But it seems like He loved them.

In the Sermon on the Mount—a sermon that predated the birth of Christianity, a sermon so profound and timeless that it would endure throughout the history of Christianity and would (in fact) shape and distinguish the character of everything Christian—Jesus pointed to lilies as examples of a splendor superior to that of Solomon's. He considered them to be better dressed than kings—lilies, that is (and a lily is one of the most naked flowers known to us). He did not apparently blush or stutter when He commanded His followers to consider them. He gave that command with the same authority that He gave the command to "let your light so shine" and the command to "turn the other cheek." It is an astonishing command—maybe given because lilies are astonishing flowers or maybe given because Jesus was an astonishing man.

After all, He had a certain fondness for sparrows and did not consider their care and feeding beneath the dignity of God—though God's care and dignity (Jesus would assert) is beyond the comprehension of men. It was God's spirit that led Him into the wilderness where He fasted and spent forty days (Mark tells us) "with the wild animals." It is easy, considering this attitude about lilies and sparrows, to imagine (and yes, this is imagination and certainly not revelation) that He spent that time romping with those creatures, not

cowering from them, and thus in His person partially fulfilling Isaiah's prophecy about a "peaceable Kingdom of the Branch."

IT IS EASY, CONSIDERING THIS ATTITUDE ABOUT LILIES AND SPARROWS, TO IMAGINE THAT HE SPENT THAT TIME ROMPING WITH THOSE CREATURES, NOT COWERING FROM THEM, AND THUS IN HIS PERSON PARTIALLY FULFILLING ISAIAH'S PROHECY ABOUT A "PEACEABLE KINGDOM OF THE BRANCH."

If this was the whole picture of Christ, we could easily write Him off as a nature lover with a heavy Hebrew orientation. But this is where the lover of lilies throws us a curve—He loved men. It was to the end that they might be saved that He came. This man who looked at flowers and loved them, also looked at an arrogant young human and loved him. He who romped forty days with the wild animals, spent and worked three years with yet a more savage and brutal species—man. He who rejoiced in God's providence for sparrows miraculously fed a crowd of five thousand people on one occasion and three thousand on another. His attention and affection was not won by the attractive and the beautiful—His glance and His love made things and people attractive and beautiful. The touch of His hand would give sight to the blind and from the hem of His garment flowed healing.

And even if someone would (and why should they) doubt the accounts of His miracles, I can testify myself I had never seen a lily until He showed me one. I had never heard a sparrow until His voice unplugged my ears. I had never known love until I met Him …and He is love.

So, all those things He did that we call "miracles" became believable to us because Christ, who performed them, operated out of love—and love (His love, at least) has a height and depth and breadth and length that reaches beyond the dimensions of mere reason. And while reasons may be found within His love, no reason would be able to contain His love. It is possible that He loved lilies because He *is* love and that He feeds sparrows for the same reason. It is possible that the evidence of His divinity lies in that love—

that in light of love, miracles seem sort of unremarkable. If God can love me, the rest will follow. And Jesus Christ is, for me, the evidence of God's unreasonable and unsolicited attentiveness, His unearned favor, His incomprehensible love.

Did I forget to tell you that He loved lilies?

Fall

1991

23rd at Thirty-Two

When I was very young I was afraid of the dark. Like everyone who has that fear, I was afraid half of the time. I hadn't yet learned how not to fear what could not be seen, let alone trust that anything beyond the dark—the unseeable—could be good. It was like I had been born with a suspicion that "something out there" was going to get me and I gave rein to my always overactive imagination, which always invented just reasons for my fear.

I thought that headlights, projected by ongoing cars as they moved across the walls of my room, were ghosts. I thought that my dad's barn was the secret headquarters of the Communists and that people became "commies" (a fate worse than death) by being kidnapped by the KGB and shipped to Russia to be brainwashed and tortured. This belief put me well within the parameters of imminent danger. I was certain that ordinary birds by day became man-eating menaces at night; that rabid dogs roamed the countryside; that poisonous rats came out of sewers and that Venus Fly Traps migrated nightly to North America.

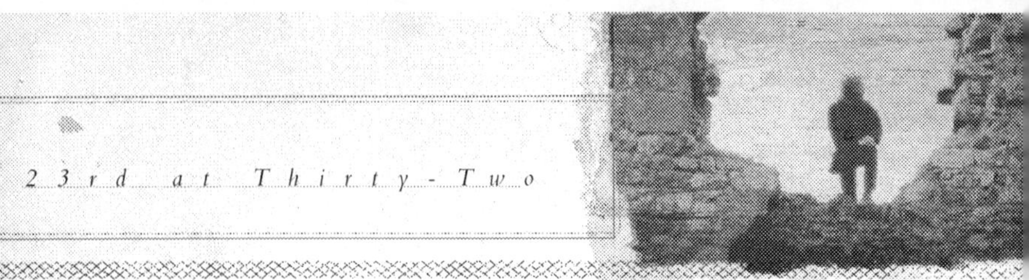

I used to recite the 23rd Psalm to and from the barn. I could say it about three times on my way there and seldom got past "He maketh me lie down in green…" on the way back. Whenever I had to be in the barn, in the dark, alone, I would repeat the Lord's Prayer, the Apostle's Creed, the Christmas story from Luke and "You'll Never Walk Alone" from Rodgers & Hammerstein's *Carousel.* The minute my work was done I would run to the house, bust through the door and pretend that I had not been afraid. I felt ashamed of those fears and was afraid that they would be with me always—even unto the end of the world.

They weren't. I outsmarted them. I became a teenager. I discovered campouts and hayrides and girls and midnight swims. The dark looked friendlier. Communism was collapsing and I found out that plants were not migratory. I found mystery where once I had known only suspicion—intrigue where I once knew fear. I "put away childish things"—I was sophisticated, and fear of darkness could not cast a shadow of shame on my new, teenaged, undaunted self.

And I threw the baby out with the bathwater. Since I had no fear I believed that I had no use for the 23rd Psalm. I thought that I did not need the Lord's Prayer or any creeds or songs or assurances. I came to think that religion was a trick people played on themselves when they were confronted with a world that was too big, too overwhelming and too scary for them. No world would be too big for me. I was young and cool and the universe was my parking lot.

And then I turned thirty. I had spent six years in college and did not have a degree. I had fallen in love and was badly burned by it. I had bills to pay and life courses to choose. I was trying to keep my head while all around me the world was losing its mind. I was faced with the consequences of my many and varied adventures...and I was alone. I became aware of my smallness and my insignificance and the world again seemed full of wonderful and dreadful possibilities. All the beauty I loved looked away from me with a terrible indifference—an indifference that left me frozen and alienated.

And one morning I was trying to hurry through my devotional time and thought it fortunate that part of the reading was Psalm 23. I thought, "Oh, I know this one well. I can skim it. I had this memorized way back when I was little and the darkness was so scary. I can pass over this quickly..."

But I could not. Because there are scarier things than the dark and

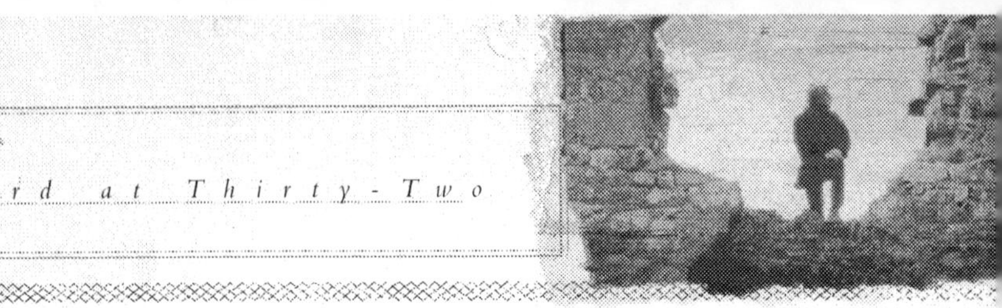

in the course of our lives we grow out of one fear and into a million others. I could not pass over it quickly because all my sophistry and self-delusion was melted away by the power of this simple statement of a faith that will not be outgrown—a truth that is bigger than the fears we invent or the confidence we affect:

THE LORD IS MY SHEPHERD, I SHALL NOT WANT. HE MAKES ME LIE DOWN IN GREEN PASTURES. HE LEADS ME BESIDE THE STILL WATERS. HE RESTORES MY SOUL. HE LEADS ME IN PATHS OF RIGHTEOUSNESS FOR HIS NAME'S SAKE. YEA, THOUGH I WALK THROUGH THE VALLEY OF THE SHADOW OF DEATH I WILL FEAR NO EVIL, FOR YOU ARE WITH ME. YOUR ROD AND YOUR STAFF, THEY COMFORT ME. YOU PREPARE A TABLE BEFORE ME IN THE PRESENCE OF MY ENEMIES. YOU ANOINT MY HEAD WITH OIL: MY CUP OVERFLOWS. SURELY GOODNESS AND MERCY WILL FOLLOW ME ALL THE DAYS OF MY LIFE AND I WILL DWELL IN THE HOUSE OF THE LORD FOREVER.

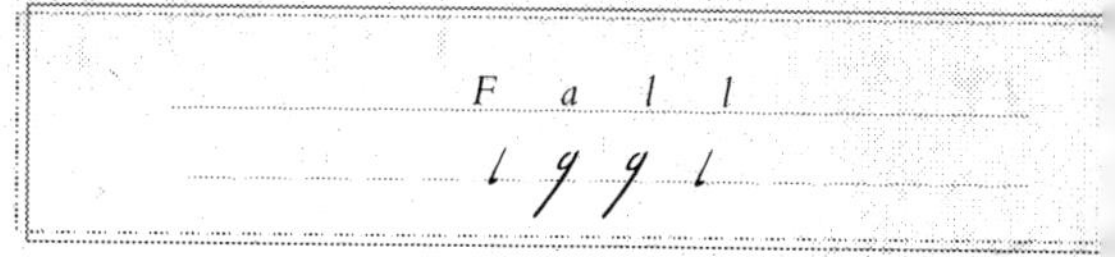

I will probably outgrow many more fears. I have lived past the luxurious years of illusory self-confidence. As I grow, I go beyond these things and ever nearer to the truth of the 23rd. I hope I still remember it when I'm one hundred.

Summer

1992

Washing at Dark

Someday I shall be a great saint—like those you see in the windows of magnificent cathedrals. I will have a soul made of sunlight and skin as clear as the stained glass panels that make their skin, and I will shine like they do now—I will shine with the glory that comes over those who rise up early and seek the Lord....

But I do not shine so now—especially not in the morning. In fact, I grimace until noon, I would never be mistaken for a stained glass saint, though at 7 a.m., I might be grey and grotesque as a gargoyle. By faith I accept that "God's commands are not burdensome," but right now, I am not grown in that measure of grace that frees me to exalt in this particular command to seek Him "early in the morning."

Right now it is dusk and far in the east the sky is already being inked with the shadow that our earth makes of itself and some nearer stars are waking there. I am in a park in Indianapolis, Indiana, and right now these great trees are casting no shadows; the greens of their leaves are holding the last rays of sun already set and the sky in the west is bright and turquoise and it shines like a semiprecious stone—as if any stone could be "semiprecious." And over all that I can see, over my motorcycle and the trunks and limbs of these hardwood giants, over this close-cut lawn and the now-abandoned tennis courts and baseball diamonds, over the sky (still fading, still and newly exquisite) and over me, a great peace washes. It comes up from the ground and down from the heavens—a deep peace breathed out by a universe that surrounds itself again by the embrace of its Creator—its God, who is to be sought by His saints in the hours of early mornings but condescends to seek out even sinners at dusk and washes them at evening in the peace of His presence and throws round their shoulders the cloak of His acceptance and puts on their fingers the ring of His pleasure—the pleasure He takes in them when He meets them here on the road even before they could get home, when He echoes in the evening the hymn He sang for them at dawn.

Someday I will rise up like the sun in the morning—someday I will shine like the saints who watch from cathedral windows. I know this, not because of any evidence I have produced of myself, but because of the witness of His Scriptures, because of the evidence of His grace, and because of the testimony of this sky that washes over me at dusk.

Fall
1992

Making/Being Made

The Bible is a very great book. It is the written witness to God's revelation of Himself in His Word: Jesus Christ. And, if you like, you can make a great deal of it.

You can speculate about it: This will make you a philosopher and people will think you are deep and very smart.

You can pontificate in view of it: This will make you a preacher and people will marvel at your courage and gift for oratory.

You can adulate it: This will make you its No. 1 fan. You can display your very fine collection of its various versions all over your house.

You can attack it: This will make you a skeptic and people will admire your honest, blind determination to live in your grim, faithless little world.

You can adapt it: This will make you a youth pastor or a Christian musician or feminist theologian or a popular author. You, too, can be the icing on a cake.

You can systematize it: This will make you a theologian and people will quote you and regard those quotes as some sort of authority.

You can criticize it: This will make you a scholar—and those who are not put off by your eggheadedness will confer on you M.A.s and D.D.s.

You can theorize about it: This will make you an expert in biblical slants on contemporary issues like political science, psychology, church growth, economics, sex and marriage.

You can ponder it: This will make you a mystic and people will turn to you for spiritual advice (and from you when they get it).

You can practice it: This will make you a model citizen—a fair, generous, and righteous (if somewhat uptight) person.

Of course, what we make of the Bible will never be as great a thing as what the Bible will—if we let it—make of us. For that which is born of the flesh—our human understanding and handlings—is flesh, and that which is born of the Spirit—God's revelation of

Himself and the power of that revelation to enliven us—is spirit. The will of man will not ultimately prevail against the will of God. It is the will of God that we should know Him as He has revealed Himself and that will has not only survived the arrogant attacks of scientific and "enlightened" men, it has (even more miraculously) thrived in spite of our best intended, though sadly misguided, attempts at "rightly dividing" that seamless robe of revelation.

So, let us press on with no faith in our own understanding and nothing but faith in the Truth that is too great to be diminished by our feeble minds and too great to not transform us. Salvation comes from God, not from our cleverness. The Bible is a very great book. Let us submit to it so God may do the great work of making us into a great people.

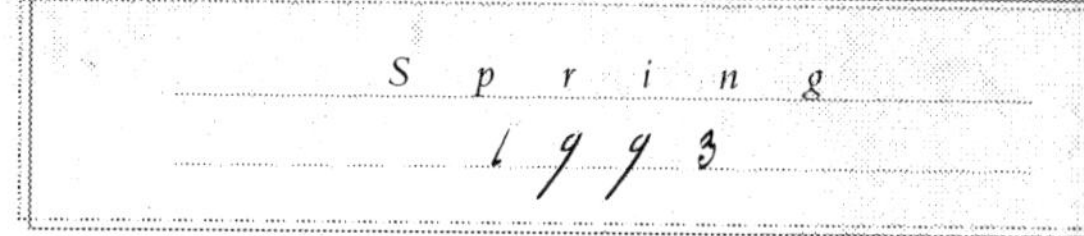

The Way We Were

Before we had stifled the cross into a symbol, before we had softened grace into a sentiment, before we had systematized the power and mystery of God's greatest revelation of Himself into a set of dogmas, we were the children that we must become again.

Every tree had hands *to* clap

and mountains had voices;

pebbles could penetrate the helmets

on the heads *of* giants....

And when we were those wee kids (you remember, don't you?) every stable was sacred because it was in a stable that Christ was born, and every star was an angel of God's presence because He had told Abraham to see in them the number of blessings to come.

Every tree had hands to clap and mountains had voices; pebbles could penetrate the helmets on the heads of giants; sins were shameful and love was irrepressible.

And we prayed powerful, profound prayers—prayers so direct and wonderfully indiscreet that we blush now when we remember them–the prayers and the faith that lifted them up to God in those heights where we used to meet Him—heights that we now view drearily and dizzily and doubtfully.

We used to pray: "Into my heart, into my heart, come into my heart, Lord Jesus. Come in today. Come in to stay. Come into my heart, Lord Jesus..." and we can't grasp it much more now than we could then, only it didn't stop us from praying. When we were little, we gave ourselves over to faith. Now we are big, and too heavy to rise above our own understanding.

When we were kids we sang for the joy of singing, we colored and cut and pasted for the fun of doing it. We ran for the love of running and laughed and got scared and saw the world as a *real* place full of *real* dangers and *real* beauty and *real* rights and wrongs.

And if the cross is more than a symbol (and it is), and if grace

is more than sentiment (and, thank God, it is), if Jesus Christ is really God's revelation of Himself and not the product of human imagination (and He is), then we will become the children we once were and must become again. Stables will be temples, stars will be guarantees, "the trees of the fields will clap their hands and the mountains and the hills will break forth in singing...." We will pray and run and work and give ourselves over to faith. And God will be our Father and His Kingdom will be our home, for we will be those children we once were, and "of such is the Kingdom of Heaven...."

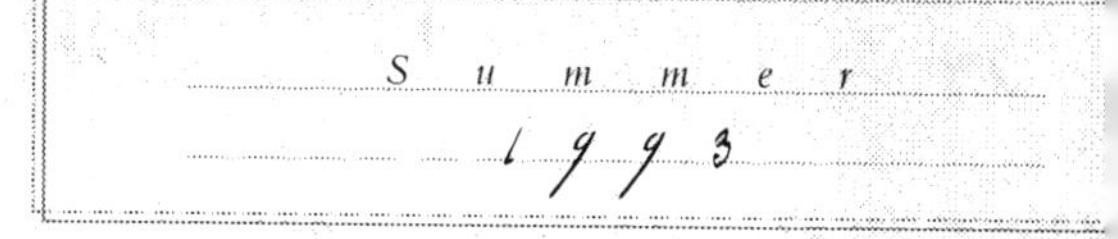

The Flight of the Philistine

It was sometime near the end of the twentieth century, somewhere between England and France on a ferry, loaded with bleary-eyed tourists and weary-looking locals, sometime in the morning—a morning that had not distinguished itself with any kind of sunrise, one that was just kind of colorless and undark.

It was near the end of that cursed Age of Enlightenment, when the supreme God of Reason had puttered out and the court of the world was cluttered with computer clowns and information peddlers, where ideas passed hands like a currency that was not backed by gold. It was where and when I met her and she was pretty and mildly likeable and this was a conversation. And although her thoughts were vague, she voiced them with something that sounded like conviction.

She said, "I don't believe in war. I can't imagine anything that would make someone want to fight another human being, let alone

kill one. I don't believe in war and if everyone wouldn't believe in it, then we could all be at peace."

Of course, you can never be sure what someone means when they talk about peace or belief or most anything else, but I wasn't too sold on the idea that disbelief in war would bring about peace. I felt kind of embarrassed—kind of Philistine. I could easily imagine wanting to fight another human being. I could imagine hunger and I could imagine (or, more honestly, I *would* remember) greed. I could imagine rage over injustice and I could imagine honest (even if mistaken) fear. I could imagine a woman two men would wrangle over. I'd like to be the sort of man two women might quarrel over. I can imagine, remember, and even presently see a lot of things that would make someone want to fight another person. And worse, I suspect that a world emptied of these things would be no more peaceful—it would just be more dead.

The person who doesn't believe in gravity is no more apt to fly than the person who does believe in it. Chances are, the person who believes in gravity (who recognizes it, studies it, appreciates its power and properties and comes to terms with them) is more likely to discover the secret of flight than the person who denies the reality of weight. They will mount up with wings like eagles while the others sink into desperate, deliberate, and useless denial. They both will dream but one will wake in flight and the other will crush himself in the comfort of sleep.

We walk by faith and not by sight—not because we are blind, but because faith gives us the courage to face our fears and puts those fears in a context that makes them less frightful. We walk by faith and not by sight because there are places to go that cannot be seen and the scope of our vision is too small for our strides. Faith is not a denial of facts—it is a broadening of focus. It does not deny the hardness of guitar strings, it plucks them into a sweetness of sound.

I don't know how that sets at the present—it probably sounds foolish—but I wish I could have said something like that (only more persuasive and even mildly brilliant) to that girl on the ferry that morning on the English Channel on this end of the Age of Enlightenment, so near to yet another century of war and longing for peace and faith and denial and gravity and flight. Maybe I'll meet her there, maybe you will. She's very pretty—brown hair and eyes and all. If you see her, tell her that the Philistine on the ferry is flying and at peace and that he hopes she is as well. Tell her, "We walk by faith and not by sight." We fly that way, too.

Fall
1993

Attics & Temples

My new apartment is in the attic of Jim and Megan's house. It's a big old one-roomer with a mind of its own—a cacophony of lines that occur at approximately 45- to 90-degree angles, with floors that sort of redefine "level." This attic has its own idea of what "square" means; its studs have their own interpretation of the classic 24-inch center.

Its walls are loosely vertical and the whole thing is about two weeks away from being much more than a lot of potential. Right now it is resistant to change—openly hostile to my ideas of what it ought to be. But slowly, surely, occasionally even patiently, I am (with the help of some friends, a hammer, a saw, some nails and a wrecking bar) enlightening it, changing its self-concept, convincing it that it is not merely an ugly, old attic—it is a great space that I would like to inhabit and be on friendly terms with—a space full of promise and beauty and order and life.

I suspect that it wants to cooperate, but it's hard and I must be patient. Whoever it was that shaped the attic before me did so with some pretty

But *we are* not wasted space,

we are temples *of a* Being

greater than ourselves, temples being built

to be inhabited *and* brought to life.

big nails, deep cuts, hard hammers, and rough saws. They considered the attic to be wasted space, storage space—a distance between the roof and the ceiling—a buffer zone and not much else. Someone else came along and closed it in for a smoking room; a place for those ignoble activities that would be inappropriate in the "house proper." They slopped over the walls with cheap, nasty paneling and put in a bathroom, covered the floors with ugly carpet and stunk it up with a tobacco habit.

Sometimes in the heat of the toil of my labor I give in to fits of selfish rage—frustration more over my lack of skill than over my apartment's progress. But late at night when I look over the piles of dust and dry wall and knee-deep debris that remain during this reconstructive effort, I am strangely moved by the place and I proclaim the Gospel to it softly. I say, "I know how it hurts to be torn up. I am often choked on the litter left by

my own remodeling. I know what it's like to settle (by the grave act of a strong will) into the despair of believing that you are wasted space. I have felt the blows of heavy hammers that nailed me to a sense of uselessness. I have been shaped by some pretty careless workers who came to the task of making me and lacked any craftsmanship or artistry. I know the pain of wanting to be changed and yet being distrustful of changes, of wanting to be worked on, but being suspicious of the intentions of the Worker. But here is some good news: He who began a good work in you will carry it on to completion until the day of Christ Jesus. However messy it may be now, however confusing and scary it appears, however endless the task may seem, we will some day be glorious, beautiful, alive! There is much tearing out to do—a lot to give up. No thin coat of new paint, no shallow, petty piety will do. It's not good enough to cover up imperfection, it must be corrected. Art, beauty, function—these things take time. They may take 'til the day of Christ Jesus.

But we are not wasted space, we are temples of a Being greater than ourselves, temples being built to be inhabited and brought to life. Though we may not understand the process, our Rebuilder does. We are His workmanship and the place where He lives. Little attic, do not despair! I'm being made by a Master Carpenter. I'm learning a little about building, too.

Winter

1993

Boats & Burning Bushes

The word *sacrament* is a non-biblical word used to describe something that may be loosely or strictly biblical. It comes from the Latin *sacramentum*—a military oath of allegiance taken by a soldier, an oath that bound him to his mission, his post, his commander, etc. Common usage has kind of distorted the word *sacrament* (much as it has the meaning of other words—like *love* and *anointing* and now *family*), but if we look back—if we dare look back—we may find some power behind this word.

If we look back—say, to the prophet Isaiah—we can see God describing Himself as a warrior—a soldier sworn to waging peace, expanding the borders of justice, armed with love and truth. If we dare to look back, we may even see God not as this nice, passive, passionless "Breck lady"-looking mystical thing, and we may discover a maniac God, a God who is wild and ferocious, uninhibited by our arrogance, unafraid of any cruelty—a God who is passionate about people, One who would truly go to hell and back out of love for us.

And if we dare look back, maybe we can then look around and see

all the oaths of allegiance through which He has shown His faithfulness to us—bread and wine and water, even frail, shadowy, little human commitment, the rainbow....

We may discover a maniac God,
a God *who is* wild *and* ferocious,
uninhibited by our arrogance,
unafraid *of* any cruelty—
a God *who is* passionate about people....

He showed His allegiance to us in the boat that Noah built, in the bush that Moses saw burning, in Aaron's budding rod, and in David's five smooth stones. We can see it in the Wall in Jerusalem, in the fact of the Bible, in every star that pierces the night, in the change of the seasons, and in every new morning....

Maybe we can hear it in the chirping of crickets or in the sound of old friends laughing, feel it in the hope and the yearning within us that will not (even when we try to note it) go away. Maybe the heavens *do* declare the glory of God, "and the skies proclaim the work of His hands." Maybe they

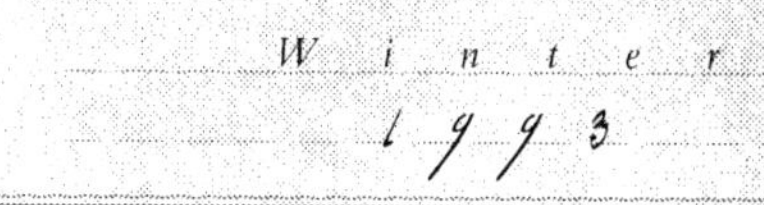

themselves are His proclamation, His declaration, His sacrament to love.

Some of us say that there are seven sacraments, some say there are only two. Some say that there are none—maybe we're all wrong. Maybe there are countless sacraments—countless "oaths" of God's allegiance to His own glory and our hope of salvation.

There is, of course, one very great and startling one—the empty tomb and the One whose body laid in it and then walked out of it on its own two feet. Next to Jesus, maybe all the heavens and hills of earth, all the music and works of art, all the rainbows and wines and burning bushes and boats seem like tiny tokens—great as they are—and maybe the issue is not so much about how and through what God swears His love, as it is about whether or not God *does* love.

"And this is how we know what love is, that while we were yet sinners, Jesus died for us."

I hope you see the faithfulness of God in everything He has made. I hope you learn to trust that all of this is His care sworn to you. But mostly, I hope you know Jesus through whom God has wildly and ferociously loved us. I hope you know and that you become sacramental to your neighbor who God also loves passionately. I hope you leave them little doubt about His love and the victory Jesus won over hate and death.

Winter
1994

Three Things, Four

THERE ARE THREE THINGS THAT ARE TOO AMAZING FOR ME, FOUR THAT I DO NOT UNDERSTAND: THE WAY OF AN EAGLE IN THE SKY, THE WAY OF A SNAKE ON A ROCK, THE WAY OF A SHIP ON THE HIGH SEAS, AND THE WAY OF A MAN WITH A MAIDEN.

Proverbs 30:18-19

Most people dislike *their* names much like they dislike *their* noses or ears or eyebrows—it's pretty much just a symptom *of* adolescent self-contempt.

I may have liked the sayings of Agur when I was a kid because they got in at the end of the book of Proverbs like third-string players

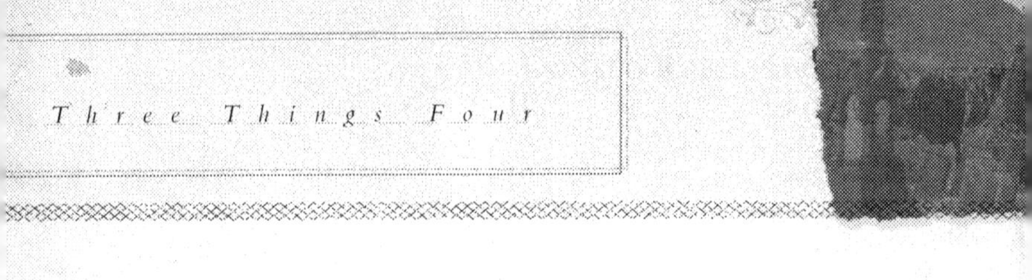

get in for a few seconds in the fourth quarter of a game that is already safe or unsalvageable. Solomon pretty much dominates the first twenty-two and a half chapters, the anonymous "Wise" gets the next seven and a half, then Agur gets one and finally Lemuel. Lemuel concentrates on wine and women; Agur focuses on song.

FOUR THINGS ON EARTH ARE SMALL, YET THEY ARE EXTREMELY WISE: ANTS ARE CREATURES OF LITTLE STRENGTH, YET THEY STORE UP THEIR FOOD IN THE SUMMER; CONEYS ARE CREATURES OF LITTLE POWER, YET THEY MAKE THEIR HOME IN THE CRAGS; LOCUSTS HAVE NO KING, YET THEY GO FORTH IN RANKS; A LIZARD CAN BE CAUGHT WITH THE HAND, YET IT IS FOUND IN KING'S PALACES. *Proverbs 30:24-28*

I might have liked Agur because he had such an ugly name. Few people really *like* their own names—not many have as much reason to hate it as did Agur. Most people dislike their names much like

they dislike their noses or ears or eyebrows—it's pretty much just a symptom of adolescent self-contempt. I just think that no matter how uninflated his ego may have been, he may likely have wanted a more flattering name—at least maybe one slightly less appalling.

TWO THINGS I ASK OF YOU, OH LORD; DO NOT REFUSE ME BEFORE I DIE; KEEP FALSEHOOD AND LIES FAR FROM ME; GIVE ME NEITHER POVERTY NOR RICHES, BUT GIVE ME MY DAILY BREAD. OTHERWISE I MIGHT HAVE TOO MUCH AND DISOWN YOU AND SAY, "WHO IS THE LORD?" OR I MAY BECOME POOR AND STEAL AND SO DISHONOR THE NAME OF MY GOD. *Proverbs 30:7-9*

Of course he came to terms with it—given his sense of wonder and his practical approach to prayer. He didn't apparently fuss over religiosity—there is nothing fancy in what he asked of God. He may have gone a little overboard with requests (considering that he says he is asking two favors and ends up asking for five) but

I suspect that God took into account his spirit instead of checking his math. Agur might have snuck the answer to his prayer into his very request—a guy with this bad math may have had no idea how much he had or didn't have, he may not have known if he was poor or wealthy. He knew only enough to ask God to be involved—to, in fact, be the focus of his life, the source of his security, the object of his desires.

It is sometimes amazing what you can find tucked away in these much-overlooked books of the Bible. It is amazing what shines through the sometimes supposed cracks. It's wonderful what a third-string, nearly unknown guy with an ugly name and a poorly developed sense of math might have to say to us.

Don't stop reading. Don't stop listening. There are many things that are too amazing for all of us, many more that empower us beyond what we can understand.

Playing Second Fiddle

There, in *that* hand,

on *that* shoulder under *that* chin—

all of *its* lightness delicately balanced

and *its* strings skillfully bowed—

it becomes a voice.

It is always important that a fiddle should remember (and, who would guess that it could forget?) that it is a fiddle—that it is wood and wire and polish and glue and not much more than that—except, of course, in the caress of a fiddler. There, in that hand, on that shoulder under that chin—all of its lightness delicately balanced and its strings skillfully bowed—it becomes a voice. There, out of the hollow body and thin skin of this little peculiarly-shaped box,

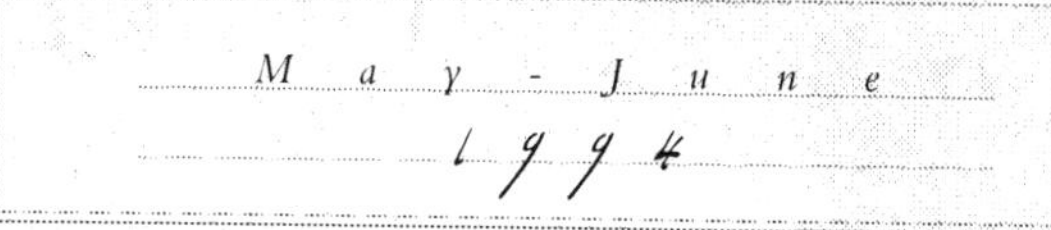

the fiddler forges his music. There, in a sense, the word becomes flesh, the fiddler's idea becomes concrete, shimmering concrete reality. And this, of course, is what a fiddle dreams of at night in the dark of its closet, in the stifling closeness of its case.

No fiddle—at least none that I have ever met—dreams of being delivered out of the aforementioned darkness to be displayed in a glass showcase. Fiddles don't have eyes—or the kind of intelligence needed to imagine a concept as foreign to them as "vision." This is why you never see a fiddle fussing over itself, primping and preening and staring at mirrors. This is why it is luckier to be a fiddle than a prince, and where the wisdom of that phrase "ignorance is bliss" is most fully shown. Fiddles do not care to be seen, so they do not mind being small, which is handy for the fiddler.

Besides having no eyes, fiddles also (and this may come as a shock to you) have no ears. For a fiddle, music is not a matter of

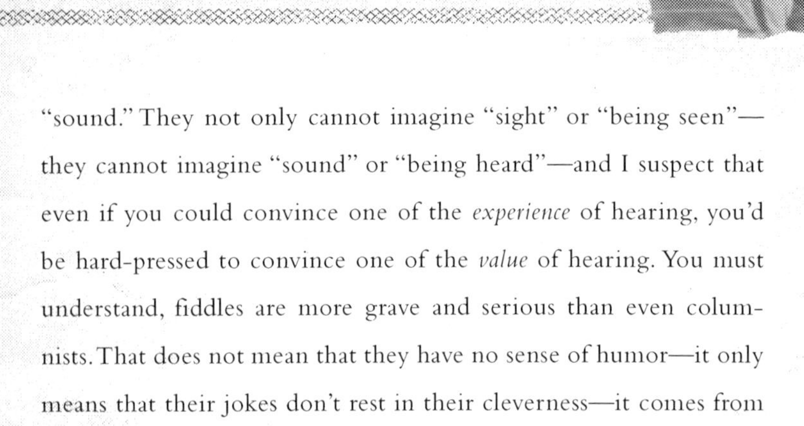

"sound." They not only cannot imagine "sight" or "being seen"—they cannot imagine "sound" or "being heard"—and I suspect that even if you could convince one of the *experience* of hearing, you'd be hard-pressed to convince one of the *value* of hearing. You must understand, fiddles are more grave and serious than even columnists. That does not mean that they have no sense of humor—it only means that their jokes don't rest in their cleverness—it comes from their lightness. And all that lightness that makes a fiddle ring would rattle to pieces any notion of the value of being an audience to one who has had the experience of being an instrument.

Now, although a fiddle may never be fooled by the folly of human thinking, very much like us, they have pain. Their necks are stiff and their nerves, their strings, are stretched. They feel the friction of the bow, and inside their beautiful brown little bodies they have only a little stick called a sound-post and an emptiness that seizes every inch of space—top to bottom, side to side. Their emptiness is for them (as it is for us) a nearly unbearable ache—an ache that is fitted to the shape that makes its tone. And sometimes a fiddle is tempted to fill that void with rags or glass or gold, even

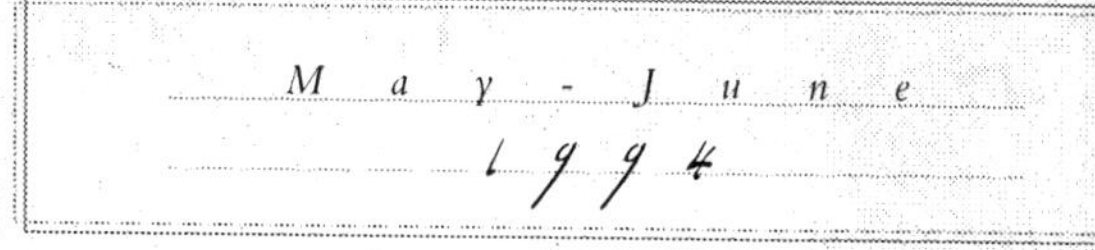

knowing that, if it should do that, it would never again resonate the intentions of its fiddler. It would never again be alive with his music. It would dull itself to the exquisite heat of the fiddler's will, the deliberate tenderness of his fingers.

And so, they resist. They resist so that they can respond.

Some fiddles have lived without eyes or ears or innards for a couple hundred years. They would die, though, if they were denied a fiddler.

Virtue Reality

Virtues are funny things. They are the fruit of faith and whenever paraded, become parodies of themselves and the worst kind of vanity imaginable. When they are not the fruit of faith they become its greatest obstacle. Virtues are most vital when invisible and most sharply imaged when they are not the focus of our attentions. They are evidence of their Source (and ours) and not the generators of it (or us).

Take, for example, wisdom. Wisdom has at its source the "fear of the Lord"—the highest regard and reverence for Him. The tendency among many of us, though, is to confuse wisdom with omniscience and to think ourselves wise in proportion to how much stuff we know. God calls us to be wise and provides us with Christ. We pressure ourselves to be all-knowing and fret over where Cain got his wife and how the earth can be as young as the Scriptures claim when geologists say that it takes millions of years more than that to produce a barrel of oil. We tend to suspect that wisdom lies in the

ability to answer imponderables rather than in Christ. And we sometimes end in self-contempt and even abandonment of our faith, not because our faith is false, but because we focused on a wisdom that is not a virtue but a vanity.

It is the same way with strength. God calls us to "be strong" and we mistake that for a call to omnipotence. We confuse strength to endure trials with an ability to walk unfrustrated through life. We convince ourselves that if we were strong we would never fail, never tire, never hurt, never need. We begin to measure strength in terms of ease of progress, equate power with success, endurability with invincibility, and inevitably, when our illusion of omnipotence is shattered, we condemn ourselves for being weak.

God has called us to be lovers and we frequently think that He meant us to be saviors. So we "love" as long as we see "results." We give of ourselves as long as our investments pay off, but if the ones we love do not respond, we tend to despair and blame ourselves and even resent those we pretend to love. Because we love someone, we want them to be free of addictions, of sin, of self—and that is as it should be. But it might be that our love for them and our desire for

It is the same way *with* strength.

God calls us *to* "be strong"

and we mistake that *for a* call *to* omnipotence.

their well-being will not make them well. And, if that is the case, their lack of response no more negates the reality of love than their quickness to respond would confirm it.

Love is a virtue and not a feeling. It is fed and fired by God—not by the favorable response of the beloved. Even when it doesn't seem to make a dime's worth of difference to the ones on whom it is lavished, it is still the most prized of all virtues because it is at the heart of the very character of God. By loving we participate in His Life and Essence. When we stoop to bait and buy good behavior we are no longer loving as God loves. We are manipulating and cheapening the dignity of the person whom we are called—not to save, not even to change—but to love. If real salvation is possible (and we know it is) it is because real love is there. And love that is real, love that is truly a virtue and not just an act—agape love—gushes from God through those who know Him. It is not strung along by those who don't.

In a world where quantitative values have obscured the reality of qualitative values—where we long to measure progress and chart growth—it is easy to give in to the temptation to judge ourselves and to try to walk by sight. But into that confused and meaningless effort God speaks with His great, still, and small voice, with His Christ. He speaks through these invisible virtues with which His people shine and in the light of their lives this desperate, smug world sees not strength, wisdom, or even love, but Him who is the source of these things and the Savior of humankind. Let us in whom He dwells look also to Him so we can shine more brightly.

His Master's Voice

If I loved my Master like my dog loves his, I would be more saintly than John the Divine…more radical than John the Baptizer…more deeply devoted than St. John of the Cross.

My dog, Bear, is a golden retriever with a more-than-weird fear of storms, an uncanny sense of how to be especially gentle around children, epilepsy, and a coat that is wildly wavy and shines gold. He has a look of nobility about him—a goofy kind of nobility—and at nine-plus years of age, he still has not grown into his feet (except his head, which is somewhat enormous). He weighs about seventy-five pounds and eats very little to maintain that weight. He loves to fetch, especially in water. He hates baths and loves to roll in…how should I say it?…stuff that smells. He knows *sit*, *down*, *stay*, but doesn't do tricks. I suspect that he is embarrassed for me that I try to show him off.

But the devout part—aside from his obvious charm—that is the part I most envy....

When a storm comes, Bear unashamedly dashes between my legs. If I lock them together, he attaches himself to whichever leg he is closest to. He does not run away in a storm—he runs to me. I don't know if this is about real safety or if it's about mere comfort, but I know that I would do better to crawl between my Master's legs in those times of storm than to feign courage or break for another and doubtless inferior shelter.

Of all the things I've had to teach Bear, coming to me was never one. I've had to teach him not to sit on the couch, not to climb into my bed, not to sit under the table at dinner—but I've never had to teach him the reverse. When my friends sit with him, if he gets nervous or upset (and he doesn't much) they play an album of mine or give him one of my sweaters to nuzzle. Bear not only loves me, he loves my stuff like I should love God's "stuff"—His church, the Bible, stars, sparrows...His voice, those things that carry His scent.

Bear takes his medicine (for his epilepsy) well, too. I've never been good at taking medicine. Bear obviously doesn't like it, but he doesn't resist—he's only slightly uncooperative. And, if I try to sneak it to him in his food, he spits it out. If I give it to him from my hand, he swallows it. I try to avoid medicine from God—even to the point of avoiding God. Bear comes up quietly and sits and opens his mouth for it.

Of course, there is one time when Bear runs from me. It's when I practice the cello, and so, who could blame him? I'd run from me too, if I could. But Bear's master is not as good at playing cello as my Master is. Bear's master squeaks and squawks away at his instrument like my Master never will. I have long since given up the ambition to be as good at everything as my Master is—I do hope that my Master will not give up on making me as good at being mastered as is my dog.

Invisible Things

And there are invisible things. Like the light behind the earth that casts a shadow of it, a shadow we call night…like the sap that runs with some wildness of life in the veins of trees that we see as dead…like the impulse behind the act…like the silence inaudible behind the noise....

Like all the beyond—too great to be fit into the lenses of our high-powered telescopes and microscopes, as close to us as the ocean is to fish, too present to be discovered (or even discoverable), a thing of which we are a part and apart from which we cannot be ourselves—invisible things....

Things cut off from our senses like Eden was barred from our first ancestors—guarded, hedged in and away, things of the Spirit—angels, the will of God, God Himself, His Kingdom (the place where His Spirit lives and reigns), love…things we dream of and imagine that we remember, things we parrot and kill in that parroting—things we yearn for and curse and deny and yearn for again in spite of ourselves—as if a part of our true selves belonged to a true world and not the one our lesser selves have settled in and surrendered to...or would surrender to if not for the persistence of those invisible things....

Those things that the visible world hang from, point to, cannot quite reach, cannot quite escape. And just when our smug, agnostic loneliness settles into some comfortable, almost manageable despair, something that goes "bump" in the night or "whir" in our hearts sweeps us up out of the numbness and into that longing, that anger, that unquenchable hope that we would just as well live without, if only life was possible without it....

If only life was not part of those invisible things—winds moving leaves, temperatures that we can measure—that affect the world, pasts, futures...invisible things.

He is the image of the invisible God. He is incomprehensible to our Western minds—as He was to Eastern ones. He came from that beyond that no human mind has visited. When we try to squeeze Him into our systems of thought, He vanishes—He slips through our grasp and then reappears and (in so many words) says, "No man takes My life from Me. No man forces his will on Me. I am not yours to handle and cheapen. You are Mine to love and make holy."

In Him, the fullness of the Godhead dwells. In Him, all things are held together. In Him, we see what love is—that it originates in God and is energized by Him.

And so, we thank God for all we see. For beauty and for the miracle of sight, for music and wonder of hearing, for warmth and the sense of touch. But we thank Him more for Christ, without whom we would be deaf, insensitive, and blind to the invisible things, and there are...invisible things....

For Children Only

The woman on television had that smug, uppity look on her face and that grimly condescending tone in her voice when she looked dead-on into the camera and at point-blank range announced with ridiculous earnest something that was hysterically, ironically true:

"Miracles are for children," she said with her educated, wilted monotone—a delivery you might call deadpan if she was trying to be funny. The funny thing is, she was not.

But she was right—miracles are for children. And the truth that popped out from between those lips that sophistication had soured, seemed to stop short of the heart of its intended target, look back in wonder, and scratch its head at the unflattering set of jaws whose bite it had accidentally escaped. That truth could have been no sweeter or more true if it had been spoken by Christ Himself.

And Christ Himself did say much the same in so many words, especially if we take the idea of miracle at its most exact sense: "the

suspension of the laws of nature by divine intervention." Christ preached what He Himself called the "Good News" of the kingdom of God—a kingdom full of miracles. He Himself said that in this Kingdom, the poor would know comfort—and even the most debauched hedonists among us know that if comfort is found by anyone, it is a miracle. In this kingdom of miraculous comfort, Christ said that the meek would inherit the earth (quite contrary to the law of survival of the fittest), the hungry would be satisfied (not a popular notion in a consumerist society), the pure would have vision (a threat to a world that thrives on sensationalism) and the peacemakers (not the most heavily armed aggressors) would be esteemed.

The TV lady and Jesus were in complete agreement about miracles being for children. But then the TV woman said that grown-up people, grown-up societies, do not need miracles. She said that the grown-up meanings that Jesus meant did not need the theatrical

trappings that He dressed them in—those circus costume miracles (those funny, childish gags like the calming of storms, the cleansing of lepers, the raising from the dead). She said we did not need miracles to find Christ or to be part of His kingdom.

Christ said *that* His kingdom—
the world where He Himself reigns—
is for children.

Therein is the rub. Christ said that His kingdom—the world where He Himself reigns—is for children. He Himself said that if we don't need a miracle we will most likely have little interest in Him. If we are able to get along joyfully in the grown-up world of supply, demand, survival, aggression, sensations, and consumerism, then we'd probably have too low to stoop and too much trimming to do to slip through that needle's eye gateway to Him. If we aren't sick, we don't need a doctor. If we aren't lost, we don't need a leader.

But, if we can admit a need, if we aren't as all-together (as we sometimes secretly fear we're not), if we can shed our thick-skinned self-reliance and peel off that thin veneer of satisfaction—then there is a place for us in His kingdom and a fairly fat chance that we can loosen our load and slip on through. If we can find that courage…or that honesty…if we can be needy, helpless, blessed as a child....

O Lord, this is me *calling—an adult in an adult world, needing to be a child again in a kingdom for children. O Lord—can You make me that? It will take a miracle.*

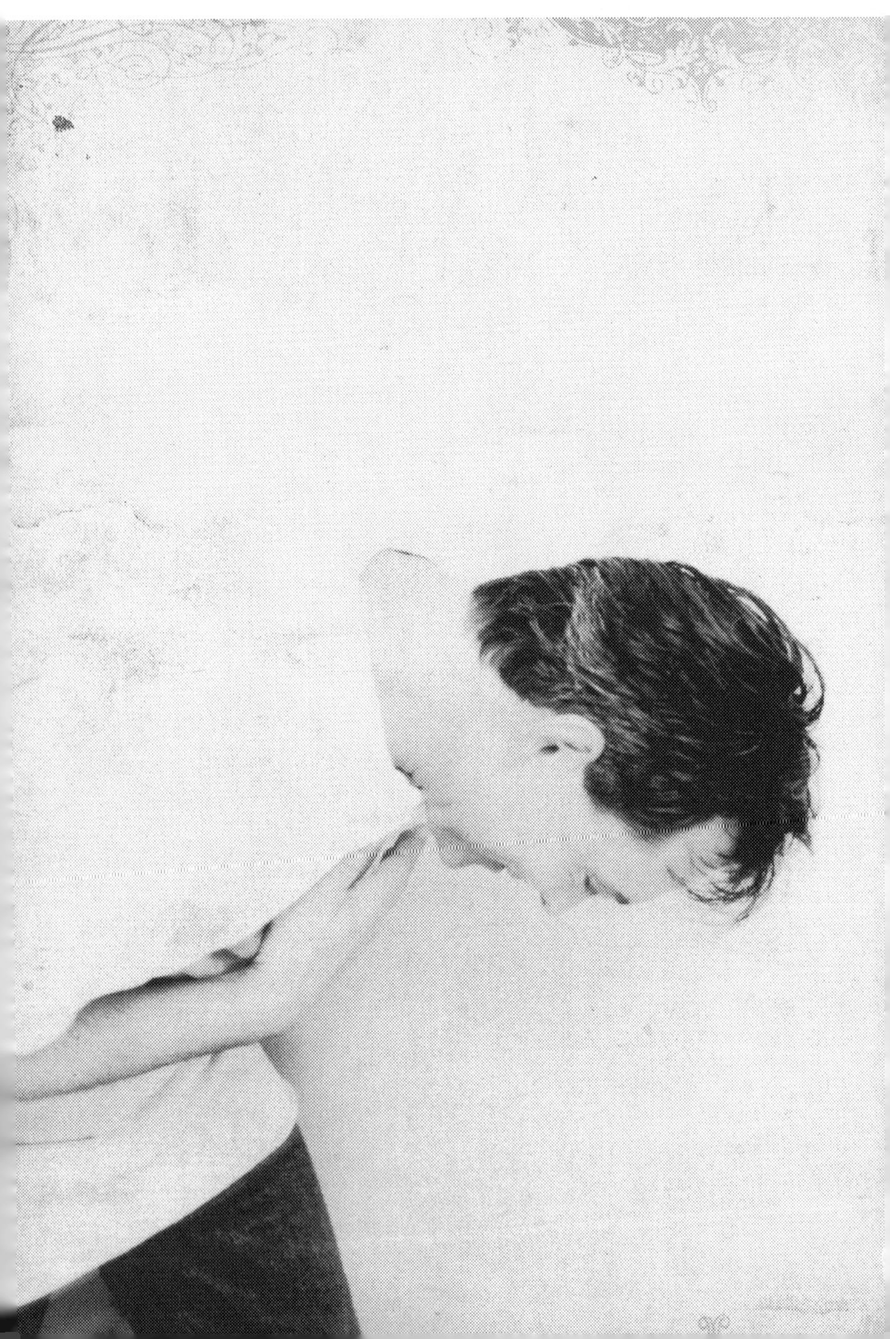

March-April 1995

Play It Again

As we age, *we* begin to forget stuff;

our joints stiffen; *our* heads go a little soft....

Getting old is part of getting past whatever

illusion we have about ourselves.

It is part *of* getting free.

My grandparents all repeated themselves a lot. Every ten minutes or so their conversations would circle and start again, word for word. As they all got older an ever broadening range of suggestions became cues for an ever narrowing range of responses: "Yes, well, did I ever tell you about that big storm we had in '39?...Do you have your driver's license already?...When did you graduate from high school?...Why is it you haven't married yet?...We had a whopper rain back in...."

So, you can probably imagine how disturbing it was to me when, after writing a column for this issue of *Release*—after sprucing and polishing it to a fine shine and faxing it in—I realized that it was a nearly exact duplicate of an article I wrote back in '93, just before "that big storm" I probably mentioned already (or have I?). Anyway, suddenly everything I thought about saying sounded weirdly like the echo of what I had already said. This, of course, would not be so worrisome to a person with a quieter disposition or even to someone who had any gift other than the "gift of gab." And, granted, imitation *is* a form of flattery, but that's only true if someone *else* is imitating you. If you imitate yourself, you just sound conceited. Or old.

Now, I am not so naive as to imagine that people have not spotted some conceit in me. I know it's there and that I am not humble enough to extinguish it or clever enough to disguise it. A person can overcome conceit though, through prayer and service and devotion. But no amount of fasting or Bible memorizing or church attending will hold sway over aging. If we live long enough, we will get old. And as we get older we will more and more repeat ourselves, as I have already begun to do. Repeatedly.

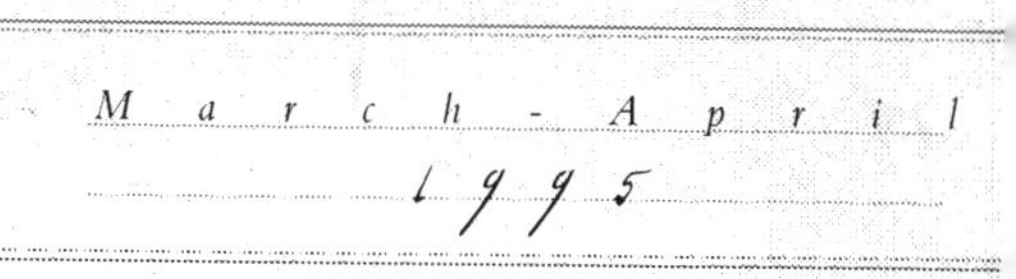

Not that I am a card-carrying member of the youth cult. I was awful at being young. My adolescence was riddled with that angst-ridden morbidity that seethes with crushes, complexes, and bad poetry. The "twenties" were the March of my life—in like a lion, out like a lamb. They were predictably turbulent early on and dissolved into quiet desperation just before passing. At thirty, I was relieved of the responsibility to be "young and foolish"—I was not yet old and I was not still young. And God, who is good through all ages, had landed me at last in a place of relative peace and even prosperity.

Of course, just as I wasted my youth by being too goofy, I blemished the high noon of my life by becoming a bit (this is so embarrassing), conceited. It's normal, I guess, but embarrassing nonetheless. And so, God, being good still, is doing what He does, doing what I can't do and undoing what I have done.

God lets us struggle and lets us prosper—we don't all struggle and prosper the same, but we all do both to some degree. And when we have done enough to think more highly of ourselves than we should, God lets us age. And as we age, we begin to forget stuff; our joints stiffen; our heads go a little soft. We drive slower and are less driven, are more embarrassed but less likely to die of that embarrassment and more likely to die of natural causes. Getting old is part of getting past whatever illusion we have about ourselves. It is part of getting free—free from reasonable doubts, irrational conceits, false securities, displaced affections....

And so, let me grow. Let me grow old. Let me grow free. Even if I have to repeat myself to do it.

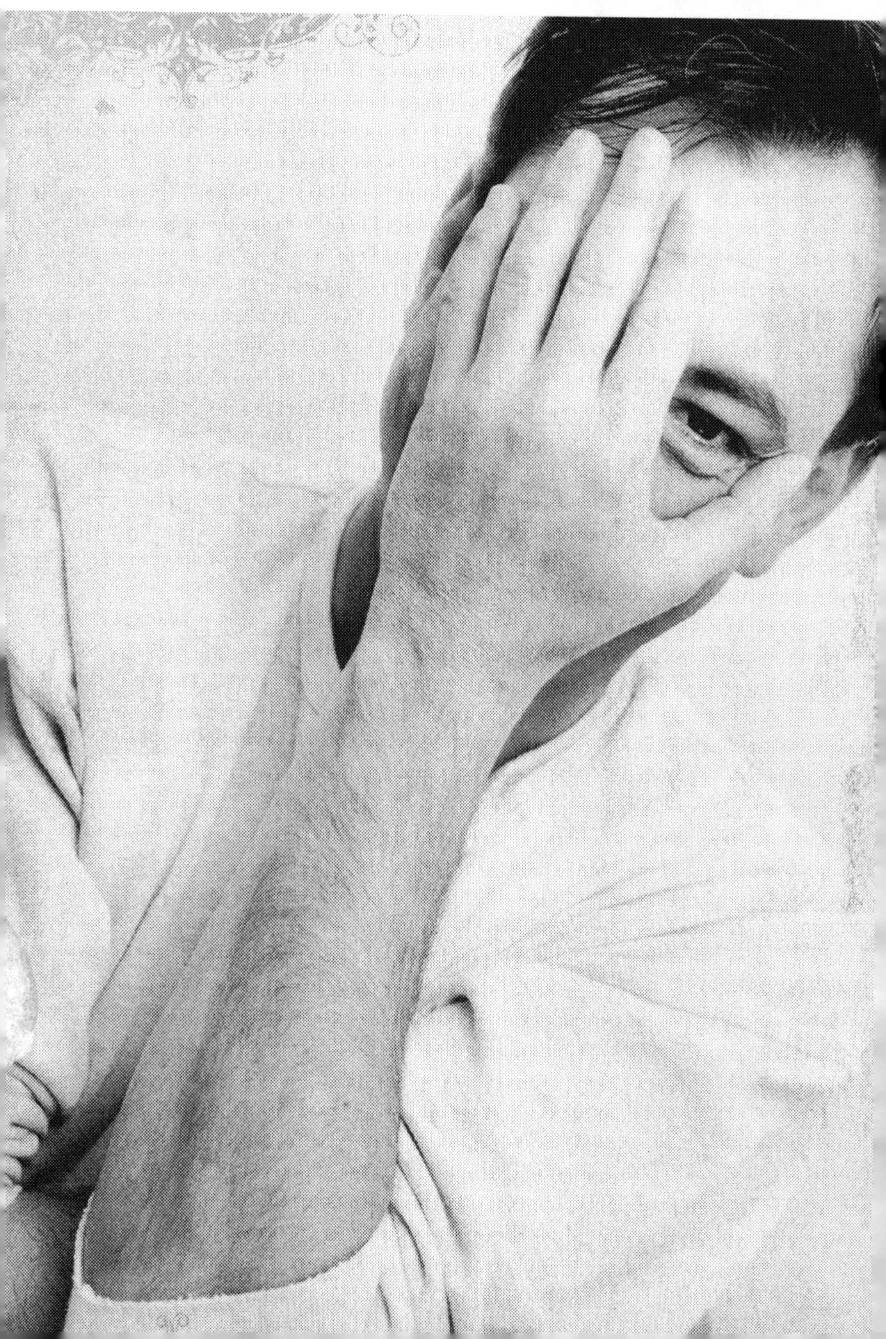

May-June
1995

Pictures in the Sky

There are those skies—skies stretched so tight you just know they're about to pop—skies in whose seamless blue reaches, you hear the snap of sails full of wind, sails moving ships like these skies move you, like these skies move oceans, worlds, time...skies stretched tight like balloons at birthday parties, full of breath, light like helium, so light you have to tie them down.

There are skies like that—skies so light they look like they could easily be lifted away, so light they seem almost to lift you, to suck you out of the grip of gravity.

But it is the sun they lift, these skies—skies into whose perfectly arched and balanced heads any sun would rise and find room therein to shine. These skies stay poised, enormously gentle, like giants across whom children climb and crawl and play—giants who are strong enough to feel the touch of these little ones and not move one muscle to risk unbalancing or frightening them.

There are skies like that. You have to look up to see them. You cannot find them beneath you or within you. They are "out" there...they are "up" there.

There are these skies—skies stretched so tight you just know you're about to pop standing beneath them. Your lungs may burst from breathing their sizable air—air from their cool heights so tall they scrape the footings of Heaven—skies so pure and strong that God built His New Jerusalem on their back. And they reach up toward that Holy City like Romeo scaling the forbidden wall beneath Juliet—skies that go endlessly, nearly forever with the beauty of her face, the quiet, unshaken gaze of her eyes, skies alive with all the virility and tenderness of young love—skies as ancient as time, as innocent as babies held in the Hands of Eternity.

And I was trying to think of how I could encourage you—of what I could say to spur you on, just trying to come up with something. And then I was overcome.

And you might say, "But it's just a sky"—but you could say that only if you'd never seen it. And you might say, "Oh, the sky is just a metaphor and he's really overcome by something spiritual, like,

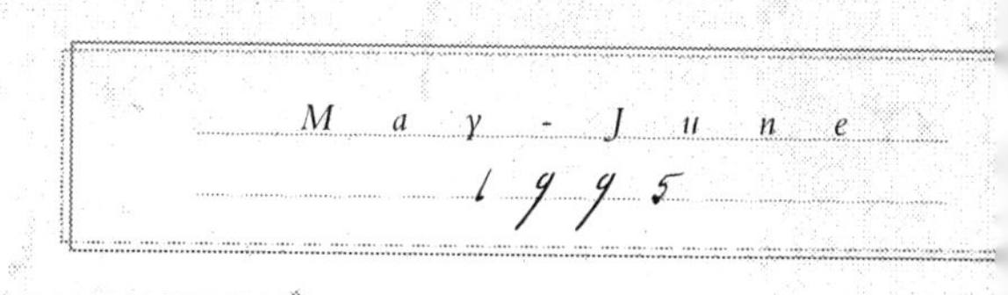

say, the love of God." But if the sky is only a metaphor, it is God's metaphor, and if you'd look up—if you'd just look up…well, I haven't the words, but....

There are those skies—skies stretched so tight you just know they're about to pop....

The Sound and the Worry

We are surrounded by—we are dependent on (and weirdly, quite even indebted to) a hundred million things that are just beyond our reach and completely beyond our control: things like favorable weather; the honesty and good intentions of those people among and with whom we live, work, and play; balanced budgets; tomorrow and tomorrow in its creeping, petty pace; our next paycheck; dependable machinery; our next breath.

A hundred million things. All of them are just as real as they are invisible, just as available as they are necessary, just as likely to fall on the just as on the unjust, as apt to shine on those who worry as on those who hope. (The difference being that those who worry are less able to enjoy things than those who hope.) But for all of us, we are surrounded by things we cannot predict, control, possess, or avoid—things that press us and compete for control—a competition that must be decidedly won by "faith" or we will be lost.

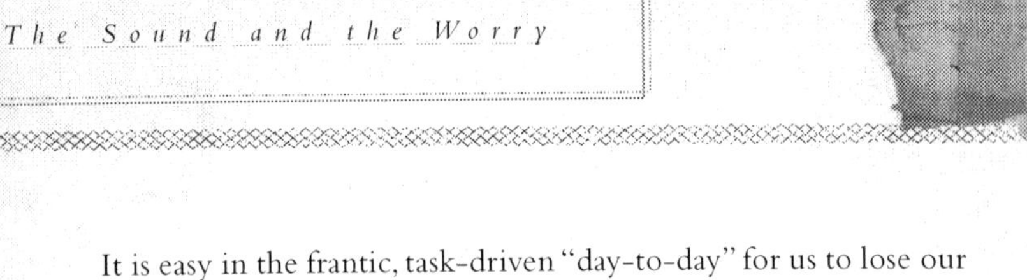

It is easy in the frantic, task-driven "day-to-day" for us to lose our "centers"—our souls—our sense of who we are and what is really important. We are haunted by the ghosts of the "what ifs" who live in the shadows of the "if onlys." They accuse us, torment us, tempt us to abandon the freedom we have in Christ.

But, if we still ourselves, if we let Him calm us, focus us, equip us for the day, He will remind us of our Father's prodigal generosity and about the pitiful weakness of greedy men. He will remind us (as He reminded the devil) that "Man does not live by bread alone," though He may call us (as He called His first disciples) to give bread to the hungry (presumably because man cannot live long without bread). He will remind us about the cares that burden common people, the illusions that blind those the world calls "lucky," and the crippling effects of worry. Then He will give us hope—hope that stretches us (where worry bent us) and faith—faith that sustains us (where greed smothered us) and love—love that is at the bottom of our deepest desires, the loss of which is at the root of all our fears.

The other night I dreamt that I was stuck in an airport terminal—another canceled flight; another long, anxious wait. The place

We *are* haunted *by the* ghosts *of* the "what ifs" who live in the shadows *of* the "if onlys."

was packed with stranded passengers and misplaced luggage, and I sank into a chair by the phone booths, waiting for the oxygen masks to drop out of the ceilings (it was a dream, remember). Suddenly, I noticed this distressed man, sobbing, pulling his hair out by the handfuls and so I leaned over to ask him what was the matter and if I could help.

"What's wrong, sir?" I asked. He grabbed yet another handful of his hair and sobbed, "I'm afraid I'm going bald!" And so it goes. We are surrounded by a million possibilities, all of which remind us that we are not the "captains of our own fates." As we face these possibilities, let's remember who our Captain is. Let us not be made captives of worry.

September-October 1995

The Divine Obsession

PLACE ME LIKE A SEAL OVER YOUR HEART, LIKE A SEAL ON YOUR ARM; FOR LOVE IS AS STRONG AS DEATH, ITS JEALOUSY UNYIELDING AS THE GRAVE. IT BURNS LIKE A BLAZING FIRE, LIKE A MIGHTY FLAME. MANY WATERS CANNOT QUENCH LOVE; RIVERS CANNOT WASH IT AWAY. IF ONE WERE TO GIVE ALL THE WEALTH OF HIS HOUSE FOR LOVE, IT WOULD BE UTTERLY SCORNED. *Song of Songs 8:6-7,* NIV

It is said that Solomon was the wisest man who ever lived, and it is often guessed that he wrote those lines—not that it would take a great genius to come up with them, but, given our twentieth century fears and insecurities about love, all of our ridiculous attempts to achieve and /or sustain it, it is a wise person who knows the beauty, the power, the value of a thing that cannot be bought and cannot be extinguished.

These few, simple lines outweigh the volumes of magazines, manuals, and marital aids that tell us that love is weak, fickle, and manipulable, that tell us that love is something we generate, something that looks very much like us. We are weak, fickle, and manipulable—love is not. Love is something God generates—it looks very much like Him.

We *are* weak,

fickle, *and* manipulable—love *is* not.

Love *is* something God generates—

it looks very much like Him.

But what does God look like?

Back in the '70s when it became "cool" for Christians to read and write books about sex, I read (of course) several such books. One of those books dismissed the medieval notion that Song of Songs was allegorical. It suggested that since Thomas Aquinas and Bernard of Clairveau, etc., were not "cool" enough to have been living in the 1970s and since they were celibates (and certainly celibacy is uncool and unsexy), they were naturally too hung up to see that Song of Songs was obviously merely an erotic poem. Now that sex was okay for Christians, we could finally admit that inflamed love, impassioned love, "erotic love" was the subject of Solomon's wonderful work. Godly love, "agape love" was okay, too—but it was stable, rational, intellectual, and obligatory.

But now I wonder....

Could it be that God "feels"? Could God be capable of passion? Could God be excited or must He be austere? Are we comfortable with the image of God as Father and nervous about God as Lover (some of us even prefer God as Parent—less a personality, more an ideal). Are we happy to have God be the Creator, but scared to think of Him as being Creative? Do we like God being an engineer, but balk at His being an artist? Does His being a logician comfort us, but His being a poet threaten us? Do we enjoy the glow of God's light but shade ourselves from the heat of His flames? Does the idea that Jesus tolerated the sinful woman's anointing of His feet and John resting his head on Jesus' breast make us squirm, so the thought that Jesus enjoyed this makes us sick? How is it that we can accept that Moses saw a bush that burned and was not consumed, yet we doubt that God can love in a rage and never cool?

Could it be time to reread the Song of Songs, to rethink our images of God, to experience again the love of God? I think it must be. I hope it's not too late.

November-December

1995

The Big Four-Oh

At eighteen, *if you* have oversized aspirations,

the whole world sees you *as a* dreamer.

At forty, you get *a* reputation

for being *a* visionary.

By the time you get this issue of *Release* and read (if you do read) this little essay of mine, I will have celebrated my fortieth birthday. In my mid- to late-twenties. I had some romantic, highly exaggerated notions about an early death—taking off at thirty-three—joining the company of Mozart, Foster, Jesus, and other immortals who checked out in their early thirties. But this was a party I didn't get an invitation to—a gang I didn't belong in (me not being a genius and all). So, in Chicago I had my own party—celebrating the fun of being alive as opposed to the mystique of having an untimely death.

Because, it's better to be alive than to be dead—that's for sure. And, believe it or not, there are certain advantages in being forty over being eighteen. Of course, there are certain disadvantages too, but in keeping with the spirit of the '90s, I don't mind viewing those "disadvantages" as being "challenges." Paul, I think, had the perfect take on the pluses and minuses of life and death ("to live is Christ, to die is gain"), so that having been settled, I have made out a list of credits and debits about being younger and older—an issue that didn't seem as large or confused in the first century as it does at the end of the twentieth:

At eighteen, if you have oversized aspirations, the whole world sees you as a dreamer. At forty, you get a reputation for being a visionary.

At eighteen, if you've thrown in the towel, you're called a loser. At forty, you're called down-to-earth, a realist.

At eighteen, if you play in the rain or howl at the moon, if you paint or invent or compose songs or poems, you're accused of being childish. At forty, you are praised for being childlike.

At eighteen, time fits you like a pair of pants big enough to swim in. At forty, time fits so tight you can't button its collar.

At eighteen, your sails are full. At forty, your rudder runs deep.

At eighteen, people misjudge your character flaws as being mere bad habits that they might change. At forty, people misjudge every bad habit as being the mark of weak character and they either dismiss you as being a lesson in reprobation or just accept you as a friend. Anyway, you graduate from being a missionary project into being either a lost cause or one of the gang.

DO NOT BE OVERRIGHTEOUS, NEITHER BE OVERWISE—WHY DESTROY YOURSELF? DO NOT BE OVERWICKED, AND DO NOT BE A FOOL—WHY DIE BEFORE YOUR TIME? IT IS GOOD TO GRASP THE ONE AND NOT LET GO OF THE OTHER. THE MAN WHO FEARS GOD WILL AVOID ALL EXTREMES. *Ecclesiastes 7:16-18*

At eighteen, no one knows as much as you. At forty, you begin to understand the wisdom of Solomon in his saying:

So, stay alive. "A living dog is better than a dead lion"—and Happy Birthday to all of you from all of me.

Never Alone

"No man is an island, entire of itself; every man is a piece of the continent, a part of the main." This phrase—both troublesome and comforting, yet beautiful for the power of its straightforward witness of truth—is attributed to John Donne. He may have been quoting someone else when he penned it and made this wording permanent, but even if he didn't get the words from someone else, the ideas are certainly implicit in Paul's letters and John's Gospel. Wherever it originated, this famous line has had an enduring impact on western civilization—our political philosophies, our theology, our arts, commerce, and culture.

So, what is hard to understand then is this: If we are not islands, why do we feel so alone? If we are "part of the main," why are we so often in a condition of isolation? Why is it that in spite of—or sometimes, more tragically, because of—our most gut-wrenching efforts to experience a sense of belonging and to participate in the

sharing of camaraderie or friendship or love, we experience a deep, disturbing alienation? The sense of aloneness permeates our existence. Sometimes it subtly, almost imperceptibly, crouches in the shadows—sometimes it dominates, ruthlessly marching like Sherman across every front of our lives.

Why?

Or more important (and more disturbing), why would any answer to this question give us little or no consolation? Why does "knowing why" offer so little relief? Why is it that we were created with a need for explanations that pales beside our need for belonging? Why are all the answers—so easy to get, to give, figure out, or make up—so unsatisfying, and our need for intimacy—so hard to give, to find, to share, so impossible to take—so necessary for a satisfying life?

I cannot answer this. What I do know is that—feel it or not—no man is an island, we are not alone. My failures, my successes, my strengths and weaknesses reach beyond me—they affect people around me. Whether or not I feel close, my life—every life—touches other lives. We are joined together in a responsibility to make this world a good one for all of us. Each of us warms the world or chills it inasmuch as we offer or withhold respect, hospitality, encouragement, love, or truth. In that sense we are all parts of each other's well-being or sickness, and we affect the climate that we all share.

But we are also alone. "Each heart knows its own bitterness, and no one else can share its joy" (Proverbs 14:10). We each have some identity that is separate (and that separates us) from the community. We are individuals, unique in ourselves. We are responsible for our choices, capable of amazing creativity, loved by the God who made us, who redeemed us and wrote our names—not the names given us by others, but the names given [to] us by our Creator—on a white stone to be given on the other side (Revelation 2:17).

So, let us love one another, enjoy each other's company, share in the common work, endure each other's failures. This will not cure our aloneness, so let's not ask that of each other. Let's learn to not be afraid of a very necessary aloneness. With others and without them we are at home. In both their company and our solitude we will meet God.

WICHITA
RADIAL SR

May-June
1996

Momentary Pleasures

Once in a while—just every once in a great while—you have one of those moments. They are those moments that come one at a time, with no interruptions, no competition, no phone ringing or beeping, no kids screaming for attention, no emergencies, no jamming of the lines, no log pile of ideas....

So you fold that last piece of laundry, you nail down that last plank. You lay that last brick and wash off your trowel with your fullest attention, aware of your deepest joy. You sharpen your lawn mower blade and savor the motion and sound of the file sliding roughly and at just the right angle along the cutting edge. You toss one extra pass of your football with your kid or your dad or your friend, you fine-tune your guitar, you reread that last couple of pages of your favorite book, you measure out and keep the safe space between you and the car ahead....

Not often, but every once in a while you have that perfect kind

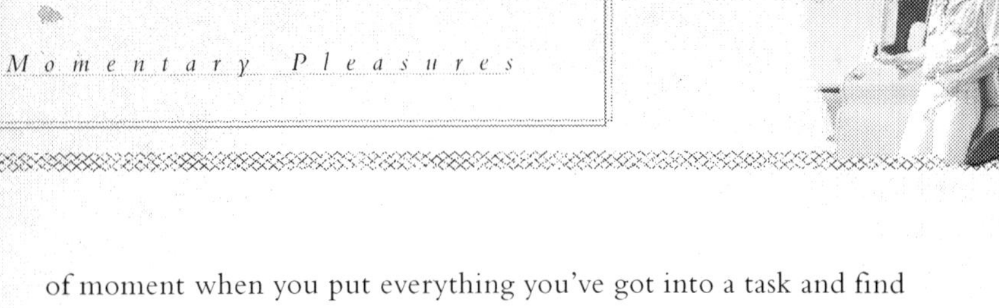

of moment when you put everything you've got into a task and find you have enough, and you feel that, even if you bungle the job, there is little at stake. You sink your teeth into something, put your heart into it, act deliberately, by choice—not by coercion of immediate necessity. You mean what you do as if there was no meaning at all in everything else—you do it for the joy of doing it, not just to get it done. You shoot from the hip, swing from your shoulders, and feel that exhilarating grace and balance of having found your center, or having centered yourself.

It is for those every-once-in-a-while kind of moments—far more than for those once-upon-a-time ones—that we can be most thankful. It is in those moments that we find some sense of who we are. Regardless of how grand or how common the event of the moment is, in it we see ourselves at our absolute best—focused, posed, and pure—no compromise, no ulterior motives, no self-deception, or pretense. We see what we are like when we have no point to prove or score, no bills to fit, no scrutinizing to endure. We meet again that child in us who still loves to swim naked in the cold, quick-running waters of the now—the child in us who can

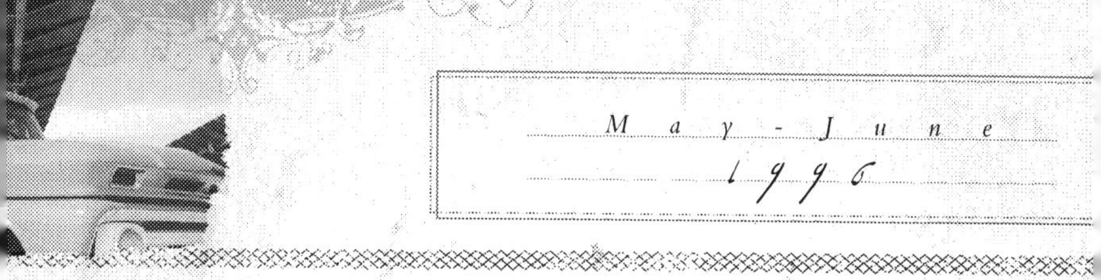

feel in his skin and very bones the warmth and brilliance of the sun. In those moments there is that flash of astonishing recognition: This is not a child who is merely in us—this child is us.

No wonder we love these moments and want them to linger. But for now they can't, so we must let them go. They are the flicker of some holy flame, a twinkling of an eye wherein the dead come alive again. Remember then, thank the Lord for them, but move on into the next moment and be present in it. It is God's present to you.

July-August 1996

Growing Still

"Moses grew and became a man. He visited his people and saw...." Exodus 2:11, besides being part of the great account of God delivering Israel out of its bondage in Egypt, gives us a few little glimpses into the character of Moses, the meaning of maturing and those microscopic miracles that play into the Cecil B. DeMille ones.

"Moses grew...." It is so nearly cliché that you hate to say it, but Moses did not come out of the womb, nor was he drawn out of the river, equipped to fulfill God's plan for him. Moses grew. This may be the best thing that can be said about any of us—not that we "have become"—but that we are continually "becoming." Growth is a sign of life, and if Jesus said that He came that we might have it, it must be good.

Moses' growth did not happen as we might wish: After "becoming a man," he was still seized with rage, fear, and all those things we'd rather outgrow. These flaws along the way make it difficult to measure growth,

and that difficulty makes it tempting to give up. But to give up—to refuse to grow—is to die. That's maybe why Christ said not to judge.

"...and became a man. He visited his people...." The mature person is one who is ready to see himself in a context bigger than himself. Many of us want to imagine that we need to find ourselves—a notion that may be true in a limited sort of way. Many of us think that we must define or invent ourselves—possibly equally true but in an even more limited way.

Moses' growth *did not* happen
as we might wish:
After "becoming a man,"
he *was* still seized with rage, fear,
and all those things we'd rather outgrow.

When Moses visited his people he was beginning to accept himself, not just as an Egyptian prince, but as the heir to something far greater, far grander than a crown. He was beginning to accept himself as being part of a people (in his case, a "chosen people"). The identity given him by the palace occupants could never give him what everyone needs—a sense of who we are. As a man, maybe he had outgrown his reputation and become restless among peers. So, he visited his people and began to know himself.

"...and saw..." In Carl Sandburg's *Rootabaga Stories*, the Potato Face Blind Man plays an accordion and wears a sign that says "I'm blind, too." Most of us have trouble seeing. Clear vision is blocked by ungrounded expectations (both the fearful kind and the grandiose kind), by narrowness, and by a lack of faith. When Moses "saw," he had come to a place where he was able to set aside his willfully-constructed world and enter the one that existed independently of his wishes. What he saw in Egypt would be stretched by what he would come to see in Midian, but here was the beginning of what would end with his view of the promised land.

And so, I hope you, too, will grow, though you—like Moses and me and everyone I know—may have flaws. I hope that you, as a part of a chosen people, know who you are beyond who your peers suspect you to be. And I hope you see that you recognize suffering and that you someday see the salvation for which we wait.

September-October
1996

The Communion of the Saints

In one of those especially poignant passages that so frequently and powerfully mark the Gospels and charge them with the character of Christ, we encounter Jesus and His twelve in a moment of deep sorrow followed by a great flash of glory. (And does glory ever come except on the heels of sorrow?)

Jesus has just alienated many of His disciples by telling them that they must "eat [His] body" and "drink [His] blood." This directive must have been even more startling to its original audience than to us. They did not hear it through the filter of some 1900 years of systematizing theology contrived to intellectualize and cushion us against the blow of His outrageous command. They met it head-on and felt the full force of it and they were repulsed.

Here Jesus, who was habitually pushing the margin of reason into the realms of faith, crossed the line. Here, He ventured too deeply into the uncharted territory of the kingdom of God, articulated too clearly

the good, yet disturbing news of that kingdom, and called for an obedience too radically opposite for the reasonable sensibilities of many disciples at that time. He called them to follow too far outside their well-defined comfort lines...and they ran away in disgust or stood paralyzed in terror as Jesus walked on—walked on into the blinding light of the liberation truth He had just spoken.

The twelve stayed with Him—maybe reluctantly, maybe for reasons that they didn't know. But when Jesus asked that heart-breaking question, "Will you also leave Me?" it is Peter—the impetuous apostle—who gives us the secret to the hidden heart of discipleship:

"Where else can we go? You have the words of life!"

Peter may very well have been as perplexed over the point of Jesus' teaching as those who abandoned Him, but he was not confused about the *person* Jesus. Peter might have misunderstood His methods and mission, but he was certain that Jesus was Messiah. He may have been in the dark about where he was going, but he knew that in Jesus there was light. He may have been scared nearly to death by the demands of discipleship, but he knew that in Jesus there was life. Just before this confession of his dependency on and the sufficiency of Jesus, he had sunk in the storm of intimidating waves and been rescued by the hand of a Master who knew his weakness and the shallowness of his faith (Matthew 14:22-31).

There is much that we are intimidated by in our walk: doctrines that run counter to our cultures and egos, tasks that seem nearly insurmountable, the weakness of our wills and the seeming severity of God's. We can get lost in the endless debates over the mechanics of Christianity and sink in the despondency of our powerlessness to grasp the mystery of grace, but in the midst of that, we must do what the writer to the Hebrews advised and what Peter did, "Let us fix our eyes on Jesus, the Author and Finisher of our faith" (Hebrews 12:2). It is He who calls us and He who enables. His body is our bread; His blood, our drink. He has the words of life.

November-December
1996

Pretty Good Genes

No brilliantly composed picture, no delicately
balanced compromise about Him would do.
He would *not* refigure Himself
to fit their miscalculated equations or disfigure
Himself *to fit their* undersized frames.

In Matthew 16:13-19 we have the fullest account of the conception of the church (in the same way that we often look at Acts 2 as being an account of her birth). Mark and Luke give briefer accounts, but I'm not going for brevity right now; I'm looking for significance. And don't worry that John doesn't include this conception in his Gospel. He also did not include Elizabeth's conception of John or Mary's conception of Jesus.

I call it a conception because for all that we don't know about conception, we at least believe that at that moment all that we are made of and all that we will grow into, is set or founded. A conception is that moment when something unique, dynamic, and alive is defined. Something old does not change, something that never was before begins—a new possibility becomes real and takes on its own identity.

This is what happens in Peter's confession that "Jesus is Messiah, Son of the Living God" and in Jesus saying that was the defining moment for the Church He was beginning to build.

Jesus asked, "Who do men say that I am?" and at least four answers were given by at least two apostles. Those who answered this question are not named, possibly because the answers—though they might be accurate—were highly unremarkable. They originated in reason, not in revelation, and Peter's answer would knock them flat. Anyway, as soon as He got His answer, Jesus dropped the whole discussion instantly as if to say that the world He made and that would not receive Him would never be allowed to define Him. No brilliantly composed picture, no delicately balanced compromise about Him would do. He would not refigure Himself to fit their miscalculated equations or disfigure Himself to fit their undersized frames. The ideas that the world had (and still has) about Him were of no interest to Him because they were and still are irrelevant to who He was, is, and ever shall be. Maybe He asked because He knew that these answers would provide a bleak and bland backdrop against which the answer to His next question would really pop.

So He asked, "Who do you say that I am?" Here, Peter distinguishes himself answering not by reason but by revelation, "You are Messiah, the Son of the Living God!" To this Jesus answered (and here I'll ask you to endure my somewhat lopsided but maybe not altogether inappropriate paraphrase), "You blessed little Pebble! Your answer didn't come from this lost little world, but it came from back Home. Now you're a rock and on this rock I'm building my house...."

People have long tried to distinguish between Peter and this confession, but (not that we can settle that debate here) who can sever a man from his beliefs without destroying both? What is conviction if it is disembodied? What remains of a man when he is left without his thoughts? Apart from each other, both are nothing. In their union there is something that never was before—something unique, dynamic, and alive. And in this union, the stuff of which the Church is made and the thing that—if she does well—she will grow into, is set. Here at Peter's confession, the truth of Heaven connects with human experience and the Church is conceived.

And just as the heavens declare the glory of God, the Church pronounces the name of His Son. And as the skies proclaim the work of His hands, the Church testifies to the work of His Messiah. Red blood and flesh confess Jesus' Lordship, then drop the ball and are baffled by the immensity of that confession. People who are not pointlessly perfect receive an unattainable revelation and then misunderstand and betray the Truth. They foolishly divide and become divisive and yet He makes them one. They stumble and limp and sometimes turn to lesser gods and then are embraced by the One they've abandoned. As Paul says, "We have this treasure in jars of clay to show that this all-surpassing power is from God" and this confession that Jesus is Messiah still changes pebbles into rock and as long as the Church confesses, she will continue to be what is in her genes to become.

We've got pretty good genes. We'll do well to grow into them.

Scrapbook

SELECTIONS *from* Rich's 1994 RELEASExtra *Tourbook*

Christmas 1978

"When I was a kid in high school it used to be really popular to wear little buttons on your coat that said, Smile, God Loves You. And that would always hack me off, 'cause I go, You know what? God loves everybody. That doesn't make me special. It just means that God has no taste."

"I'm not an outdoorsy kinda guy. I don't chop wood in my spare time. I think a lot of people have this illusion that I live in those pictures that you see on albums, and out on the lake building a fire. The truth is—I have trouble building fires."

Rich's dog, "Bear"

"I love truck-stop breakfasts—especially cheesy omelettes and greasy potatoes and buttery toast. Waitresses are quick with the coffee and never fussy. I hate restaurants where waiters have too much style and your plates have more finesse than food."

With dad and mom (John & Neva Mullins) in 1989

"I don't think I really understood poverty at all until I met these kids—

the poverty of those who go to bed hungry and the poverty of those who sleep with indifference. Wealth can't be defined in terms of what we have, but only in terms of how free we are to give and take."

"I COULDN'T DESCRIBE A 'TYPICAL' DAY OF TOURING BECAUSE I'VE NEVER HAD ONE."

"Before I got into this music business, I was determined to live a life of dire and grinding poverty. I remember my uncle saying, 'Wow, you are so proud of being poor—what's so great? You would do a lot better to be a little more industrious, a little more frugal. If you're really concerned about the poor, becoming poor isn't going to help them, it's just going to ease your own conscience. If you're really concerned about the poor, go out and make a fortune and spend it on them.'"

At a campout on his 23rd birthday. (October 21, 1978)

"So, this minister came in one time before a concert, and after about three minutes of quiet he said, 'Well, do you guys want to pray?' We all felt stupid for him because we were praying."

Beaker & Wife

"After hearing yourself night after night, it's hard to imagine that anything you'd have to say would be worth listening to."

"At the 'Y' today, this one guy who is usually very friendly talked a little bitterly about how I seem to have it so good. I suppose I do, although I sometimes feel like it is more than I can handle. I guess the grass is always greener.... I think I would envy me too, if I didn't know me better..."

"People often ask me if I get nervous before a concert. Well, I don't. I get excited, kind of anxious and thrilled all at once.... The best that can happen is that someone can catch a glimpse of the glory you're hinting at. At worst you will make a fool of yourself".

Full Name: Richard Wayne Mullins

Favorite Bible Passage: Isaiah 40

Hidden Talent: I can pop my hips out of joint…way cool.

Life's Greatest Challenge: I can't work a calculator or balance a checkbook, so I don't have a checkbook or a calculator.

Best Gift Ever Received: The bird feeder and bird watching book from my parents

Best Advice Ever Given: From my dad, "If you can live without her, do."

Favorite Classic TV Show: *Bonanza*—My parents wouldn't let me watch it 'cause it was on too late, but I'd sneak out and lay at the top of the stairs and listen.

Most Memorable Meeting: Having Phil Keaggy introduce me to Mark "Grand Funk Railroad" Farner

Cartoon Character That Reminds You of You: Elmer Fudd

Word or Phrase you Most Often Overuse: *Way.* I say it way too much.

Best Part of Your Childhood: Taking a bath, putting on my pajamas, eating a bowl of cereal while watching one last television show before having to go to bed.

Best Part of Staying in Hotel Rooms: You always have clean sheets and never have to make your bed.

Worst Part of Staying in Hotel Rooms: Trying to figure out how to set the alarm clock

Favorite Book: *Orthodoxy* (G.K. Chesterton)

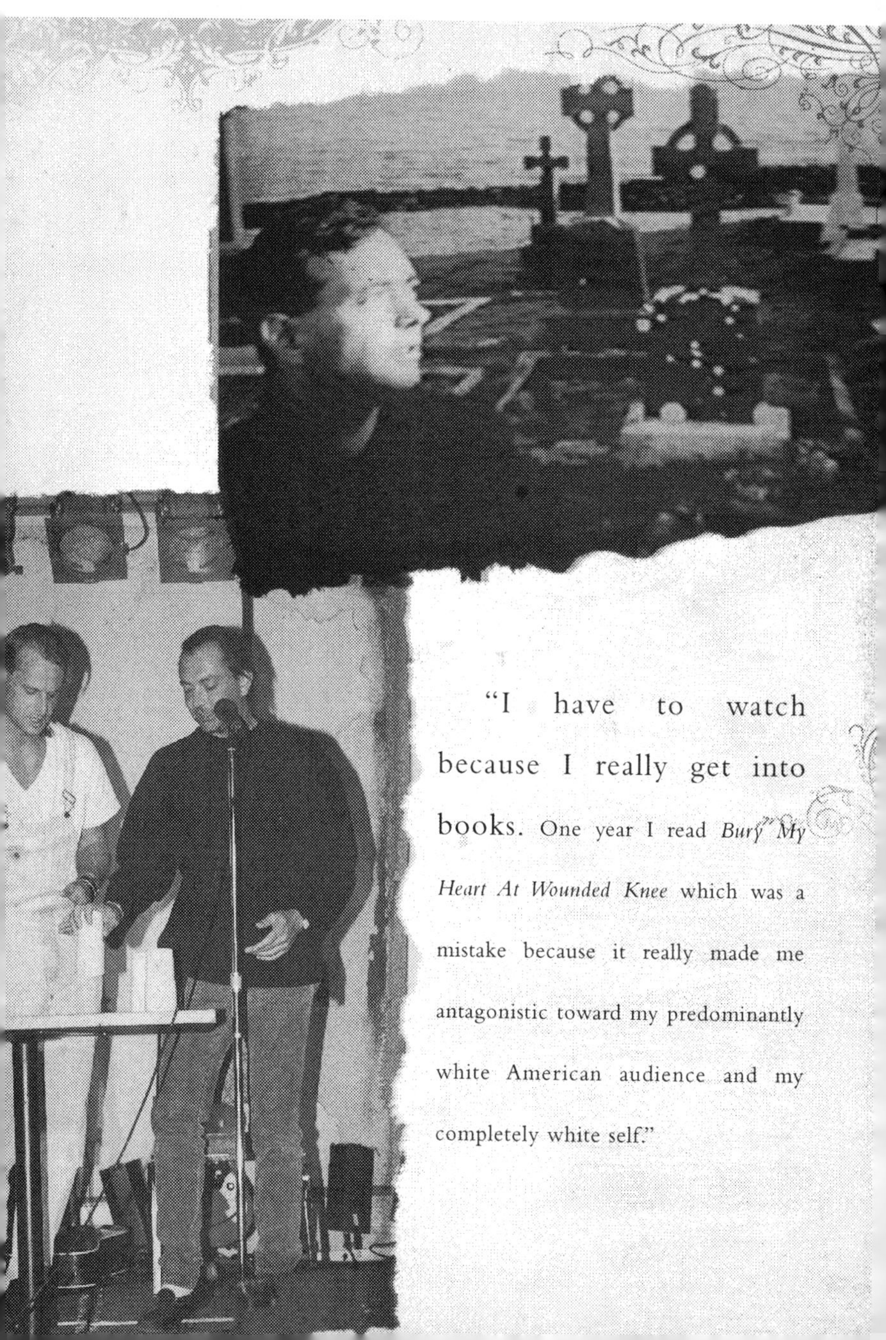

"I have to watch because I really get into books. One year I read *Bury My Heart At Wounded Knee* which was a mistake because it really made me antagonistic toward my predominantly white American audience and my completely white self."

Poet Cornered

Over the last decade, Reed Arvin has been privileged (by his own admission) to be both friend and producer to Rich Mullins. He was there when the first tentative chords and vocals were laid down on vinyl (it was ten years ago, remember) and in 1996 he's still the man at the helm for Mullins' latest, *Songs*, an aptly titled retrospective of some of Christian music's most popular songs as penned and performed by everyone's favorite ragamuffin.

Arvin has also sat in the producer's chair for artists 4HIM and Bruce Carroll and has been composer of some snappy ditties for television commercials. His talent even extends into the written word, as evidenced in his popular first novel, *The Wind in the Wheat*, the story of a Christian artist's climb to and struggle with stardom. His novel's hero, who many surmise was based on Mr. Mullins himself, is in reality, the embodiment of Reed's experiences working within the Christian music industry. As for Rich, his story is probably most easily found in the songs he writes, as Reed Arvin has discovered each and every time he's worked by his side. There's a Bible story that reminds me of Rich Mullins. Maybe you remember it: early in the book of Acts, Peter and his buddies are preaching within earshot of the Sadducees. Peter, not known for his tact, is stepping on toes, both social and political. He's calling spades spades, and the spades don't like it. In fact, they want it stopped. So the Sadducees call Peter and his pals into a big meeting, and give them a funny kind of order: "Look," they say, "you can believe whatever you want, but would you just shut up about it?"

This, my friends, is a sentence often uttered to Rich Mullins. Not by Sadducees, of course—by record company reps and even by producers, like me. "Do you have to talk politics in your concerts?" "What, may I ask, do oil companies have to do with the Gospel?" "We all know televangelists are mainly crooks, but did you have to name names?" In other words: "Rich, you can believe whatever you want, but would you just shut up about it?"

Shutting up, thank God (and I mean that quite literally), is not what Rich Mullins is very good at. I've always believed his gift is only part music; the other part is pure prophecy, and it's a gift that lies uneasily on its recipient. Prophets aren't necessarily the best party guests. But if Rich Mullins were better adjusted and better behaved, a lot of art would not exist in this world, and a lot of truth would still be unspoken. A lot of the songs that you and I have been ministered to by would still be thin air. Of course, with all those toes getting stepped on, it also must be said a lot of hurt feelings would never have needed repairing. Maybe even a few enemies would have remained unmade. But prophets occupy the space between the risk and the payoff and that's where Rich Mullins lives.

If Rich Mullins *were* better adjusted
and better behaved,
a lot *of* art would not exist in this world,
and a lot of truth would still *be* unspoken.

To tell or not to tell? What would you do? Suppose you had this crazy gift, this prophetic vision that compelled you to be the one to point the finger, to tell the tales. Would you want it? Or would you shirk it, preferring to be liked by all rather than sincerely admired by a few?

At least in Rich Mullins' case, he gets to tell his tales with a song, and that dulls the blade even while it sharpens the truth. There's comfort in the poetry—a place to hide in the beauty of language. After all, he's pointing the knife at himself most of the time, anyway. If we get cut, it's from shrapnel, not blades. Rich Mullins of the exploding songs....

Songs are where Rich's greatest gift resides, even though he is a powerful communicator in other ways. It's in the songs where whatever message God has chosen to flow through Rich greets the world. And after eight albums, it was high time to put together a compilation—a collection of work that represents the best of some very fine, highly explosive writing.

But putting together a collection meant making tough decisions. How could we pick which ones to include with so many options? Only twelve could make the grade, with three new songs added to put punctuation on a long musical sentence. Here's how record companies normally make that choice: they make a list of all the radio hits; they take the ones that charted the highest and they're done thinking about it. But when they made a list of Rich's singles that charted in the top five, there were twenty of them, so that didn't help. Choices had to be made.

Maybe your list would have been different. But how could you leave any of the ones that are on the project off? Could you do without "Creed"? Could you abandon "Awesome God"? Forget "Sometimes by Step"? Or "Hold Me Jesus"? See what I mean? In the end, all the songs on the disc remained because there was no way to cut them. They mean too much. And you could, perhaps, make another complete disc with different songs that mean as much to you. But CDs only hold so much music.

Recording new songs on a *Best Of* is always a little tricky. After all, you've already put together your finest work, and anything you add to it needs to be at least as good; you hope, of course, that it will be even better. It's a chance and a challenge to show what you've learned. And there's the record company, too—they want more radio hits. But radio singles are usually picked from a disc full of new material. With only three new songs added on Rich's project, there wasn't much margin for error.

As usual, Rich wanted to do something different. Two of the new tracks on *Songs* aren't really new at all: "Elijah," from his debut album, is a song that many people feel is Rich's finest ever. But when we did it the first time, we were a couple of bums trying to figure out which end of the microphone to plug in. "So let's record it again," Rich said, "but bring it up to date a bit." Agreed. One down, two to go.

"Sing Your Praise to the Lord" was the first song Rich ever had professionally recorded, if you can imagine that. The song of the decade. The song that sky-rocketed Amy Grant's career. A cornerstone of Christian music. And that, of course, was why we argued over it. I didn't want to record it. What can you add to a classic? But Rich revealed a secret: there was a long middle section that had never been heard before that Amy's camp had neglected to include. Rich wanted it unveiled. So a new, acoustic guitar-driven version of possibly the most famous song in contemporary Christian music made the disc. Two down, one left.

"We Are Not As Strong As We Think We Are" is a different kind of song for Rich; it's an unabashed love song. Different, yet the same; the same passion and fragile humanness are there, exposing more, perhaps, than the composer would have wished. If you ever wondered what kind of song Rich Mullins would write you after you broke up with him, this song is the answer.

And so the tradition continues—what most of us shut up about, Rich speaks. It gets him in a lot of trouble, but it gets him a lot of adulation, too. And caught in that tension he keeps on, taking his place in a treasured line of artists who speak the unspeakable.

So the disc, *Songs*, is a history of writing and singing and arguing and winning and losing. What does it all mean? The songs will mean something a little different to each one of you. What it meant to me to be on the other side of the glass as Rich told his tales doesn't fit in a sentence or two—not after eight records.

There is a space on the liner notes of every album for the producer to write his personal thanks. I didn't say much this time because I didn't know what to say after so long. So I'll say it now: *Rich, thank you for sharing too much. You turned your wounds into art, and I'm grateful. You'll find your peace when art has a name. Until then, may your quill never run dry.*

Ben Pearson is a photographer/filmmaker originally from upstate New York. He currently resides in Nashville, Tennessee with his wife, Elaine, and their three children. He considered Rich a dear friend for many years.

The images appearing in this publication were photographed in Ireland; Wichita, Kansas; Window Rock, Arizona; and Nashville, Tennessee.

Photograph of Ben Pearson by Jimmy Abegg

Printed in the United States
by Baker & Taylor Publisher Services